REINCARNATION & KARMA

Albert Bodde

REINCARNATION & KARMA

Translated from the Dutch by Jill Penton

Index compiled by Lyn Greenwood

SAFFRON WALDEN
THE C.W. DANIEL COMPANY LIMITED

First published in The Netherlands in 1997 by
Uitgeverij Ankh-Hermes bv, Deventer

This English-language edition published by
The C.W. Daniel Company Limited
1 Church Path, Saffron Walden,
Essex, CB10 1JP, United Kingdom

ISBN 0 85207 326 7

Produced in association with
Book Production Consultants plc,
25–27 High Street, Chesterton, Cambridge, CB4 1ND
Typeset by Cambridge Photosetting Services
Printed and bound by St Edmundsbury Press,
Bury St Edmunds, Suffolk

CONTENTS

FOREWORD

Those who explore the subject of reincarnation and the closely associated idea of karma can discover many answers to diverse life and death questions.

Albert Bodde has made an extremely successful attempt at clearly explaining the concepts of karma and reincarnation. He does so with love and understanding. Albert asked me if I was willing to write a foreword because he knows that this subject lies particularly close to my heart.

A couple of times I have given a lecture on the subject; once for the Rotary Club. There were only a few people present then who were completely in agreement with me. After the lecture a couple of people remarked: 'This would interest my wife, I am far too down-to-earth for it.'

My reaction to this is: what a pity that this down-to-earthness keeps so many men and women away from such interesting and essential insights into life.

The lecture to the Freemasons, on an evening when the women were also permitted to be present, was better received by both sexes.

My approach to the subject is different from that of Albert. I look more closely at personal experience. For example for answers to being in love and for recognition at first sight, and into old relationships. My search focuses on people with whom I seem to share my life time and time again. And on places and cultures, wherever they might be in the world, with which I feel a connection, albeit positive or negative. Is this continual coming together somewhere an opportunity to work out a collective issue? Or is it because we owe each other a karmic debt?

However, we should not immediately identify the concept of karma with guilt. Karma can also be a strong love connection between two or more people. If you delve into past lives, via regression or spontaneously received images for example, you will discover that you are sometimes partners, sometimes parent and child, sometimes brothers and sisters. All these different relationships help us to become ever more complete human beings; that is human beings who gain insight and wisdom in all sorts of ways, in all sorts of situations and in all kinds of different relationships. Other people, particularly those most dear to us, help us by constantly holding up mirrors. Thus we evolve an even greater wisdom from all the different times and cultures that we pass through until the moment arises when life on earth, that is reincarnation, is no longer necessary.

Paul Kluwer

PREFACE

Perhaps you are asking yourself why it is necessary to add yet another book about karma and reincarnation to the many that already exist. That is a question that I naturally asked myself before giving the manuscript its final form and offering it to the publisher.

In the first place a book flows forth from the desire of the writer to express himself. His message is unique in the sense that he treats the subject in a different way from all those before him. Everything has actually already been said and written, but each 'literary' document is a personal and unique fingerprint in time and space and as such has a right to exist. This fact can make it interesting for the reader to read two or more books about exactly the same subject. I also cherished the thought that I could add something from my own background and view of life – more about this later – to the many articles and books that have already been published on this subject. Something that might in certain respects be an eye-opener or an enrichment, an addition to existing opinion.

Secondly this book grew more or less unintentionally over the years. It began with several articles that I had written about karma and reincarnation for the magazine *Prana*. I then added more generalised chapters to the existing articles and, as the idea of a book 'materialised', removed duplication from the articles and made links with the other chapters. Even so, some of the chapters have kept their somewhat independent essay-like style. This was necessary in order to preserve the originality and intensity of the initial text. Finally I hope that the reader, having pieced together the puzzle, will see a coherent, comprehensive picture before him or her.

The subtitle of the Dutch edition of this book is 'A Search for Love and Logic in Creation' and that is what the process of writing it became too. In retrospect it proved to be a far less straightforward, and less obvious search than I had expected it to be.

Moreover, I do not presume to supply ready-made or simple answers to everything related to this subject. In this sense reading this book is also a search, that we, you, reader and I, can make together.

The result of my search now lies before you: a somewhat kaleidoscopic work in which karma, reincarnation and other related questions are approached from different angles. This has made the account broader, more complex, and far more personal than I originally intended, and perhaps less vague and noncommittal too.

Without mentioning them by name I would like to thank all those who helped me with valuable suggestions and moral support during this undertaking.

INTRODUCTION:

THE FASCINATION
OF REINCARNATION

Reincarnation: for one a promising perspective, for the other an absurdity; for one a matter of course, for the other an idea from some scatterbrained theory about life and death. Reincarnation! It comes up in conversation more and more frequently, also in circles where until recently you would not dare to mention the term for fear of being considered a fool. Yet reincarnation is a reality for an increasing number of people, a real possibility. These days you can hardly open a newspaper or magazine without finding something about 'past lives' or 'near-death-experiences'. The term reincarnation comes up often and is used regularly on radio and television. But what is reincarnation, and what is its fascination? Is it a myth or is it a tangible, meaningful aspect of life? This is what we shall be exploring.

What is the fascination of reincarnation? We shall see, or perhaps not, but we are going to investigate it, to try and understand the concept of reincarnation, to attempt to make it tangible and alive.

When we talk about reincarnation it appears that we cannot avoid the idea of karma. They are like the handle and the blade of a shovel. We cannot dig with just the handle, but we do not get far with just the blade.

They are inextricably bound up with one another; one part has no significance, no function without the other. Likewise if you investigate the concept of karma, you automatically encounter the idea of reincarnation.

Reincarnation had no particular meaning for me personally until I came into contact with a book at a lecture about twenty years ago. It raised questions about the significance of things that happen in life and particularly focussed on the role and meaning of reincarnation and karma. Its title was *In the Light of the Truth, The Grail Message*. When I read this book it slowly became clear to me how essential the ideas of reincarnation and karma are, and my own approach to the subject in this book is partly based on what I discovered in the 'Grail Message'.

Let me point out that I do not think that we can yet prove reincarnation scientifically (and perhaps we never will). However, on the basis of the scientific research and experience available, and by using logical reasoning, we can *make an acceptable case* for the concept of reincarnation and that it is plausible.

While official science continues to see material reality as the only reality, no scientific evidence can be expected. Strictly speaking science is unable to pronounce upon the subject of reincarnation because it is related to the 'immaterial', and science *voluntarily* limits itself to the reality of the tangible.

Happily in recent times we see the appearance of change within science. We find scientists endeavouring to discover wider relationships and attempting to close the gap between the latest physical insights and the old spiritual knowledge. They note striking parallels between these two worlds.

Scientists such as Fritjof Capra, Rupert Sheldrake and others are formulating theories that could perhaps provide explanations for relationships and regularities that we intuitively experience as real, but that we cannot yet explain rationally.

With this book I primarily want to indicate *the importance of insight into reincarnation* when querying the meaning of our existence; when asking ourselves if there is such a thing as justice in this world that often seems so iniquitous; and finally when searching for a logical and coherent world view that can answer these questions clearly.

Until now the answers to life questions given by the Church and other religious, philosophical and ideological institutions were, for me and probably many others, somewhat incomplete and unsatisfactory. The insights lacked a clear and unambiguous logic, characteristic of sound knowledge or science, and one could often intuitively feel that false and deceptive elements had crept in. Sadly I find that the same applies to esoteric philosophy too. It has without doubt produced extremely valuable insights for many people, but it often remains vague and obscure.

I found the scientific view of the world even less satisfactory. Science can explain a multitude of phenomena very effectively but there are still many questions left unanswered. If you keep on asking until the 'final questions' are posed then even science falls silent, particularly when it is unwilling to go beyond the limits of the material.

The starting point for our exploration of the concepts of reincarnation and karma is the central idea that reality is not only tangible, material, but that an intangible, non-material world exists 'alongside'. This is a view that underpins all the religions and mythologies throughout the world. Furthermore we assume that regularities exist in the parallel non-material world and that they act in a similar fashion to the 'laws of nature' that exist in the material world, creating order and integrating the whole. Let me give a perhaps seemingly simplistic example. When I throw a ball against a wall that ball bounces back to me. This is the simple principle of action = reaction. Would it be possible for an intangible thought of mine to bring about a reaction and return to me in some form or another? This premise, that a non-material world exists in which similar laws of nature operate, is the only assumption that we shall make at this time.

This book begins with two, generalised chapters about karma and reincarnation; I then go on to consider certain aspects in more depth. It is not my intention to just put a few facts and figures on paper about reincarnation, but rather to illustrate the broader relationship in which knowledge of reincarnation becomes something precious – precious because this knowledge provides a completely different, very caring and meaningful perspective to life. Thus we will examine the relationship between reincarnation and Christianity, give attention to the great cosmic laws, look at reincarnation and karma in a historical perspective and contemplate the origin of man and the issue of evolution or creation. In the final, concluding chapter we shall complete the circle and examine the 'why' more deeply, the significance of our search.

–1–

REINCARNATION

Many of us probably already know the feeling of having met someone before or of feeling immediately at ease with a stranger. Likewise we may feel very much at home in a particular environment or situation in which we have never been before. In the same way people sometimes know exactly which way to go in a town in which they have never previously been.

Consider the story of Mrs. Heyman from London.

'In 1919 my husband and I took our annual holiday in Devon. One evening we stayed overnight in a village some distance from the main road. The next morning while we were exploring the surrounding area it seemed that the place became more and more familiar to me. One house in the village attracted me in particular. Later when we ventured up on to the cliffs that curious feeling of having been here before came over me again. And suddenly I was gripped with excitement and dizziness, and knew no more than this one thing, that I held tightly onto my husband and then fell, fell, fell...

When I came too, I was lying in the grass and saw that my husband was bending over me anxiously. "What's the matter with you?" he asked me as I opened my eyes. "You nearly pulled us both over the edge!"

On the way back to our lodgings in the village he told me more about what had happened, that I had suddenly clung to him and screamed out: "Alan, Alan, help!" As my husband is called George he found this quite bizarre and disturbing. After the meal we were chatting to the hotelier and my husband told him about the circumstances on the cliffs that had nearly led to our downfall. The man became attentive and then said that his father had once told him about a young couple that had fallen to their death, long ago, from the very spot on the cliffs that we were talking about.

"Were they strangers, who were visiting the place?" asked my husband. "No", was the answer, "they lived here in the village in the white house down there with the window displays." It was the same house that had seemed really familiar and trusted to me.

We investigated further and finally found the graves of the two young people with the following inscription: "In loving memory of Alice and Alan Johnson, who fell in an accident on 30 June 1869."[1]

Old roots

When reincarnation is mentioned most people will initially think of the old Eastern religions. For several thousand years millions of Hindus and Buddhists have believed in the doctrine of rebirth. Hinduism is familiar with the concept of Atman, the immortal self or eternal core of man that sometimes manifests in a body of flesh and blood. The image is simple: the immortal spirit puts on a material jacket. This is called incarnation, which literally means 'in the flesh'. If this happens more than once it is referred to as reincarnation.

Atman is discussed in the Upanishads, the 5,000-year-old, holy Hindu texts. The concept of karma(n) is also mentioned. In Sanskrit karma means 'work' and relates to what the Bible refers to as: you shall reap what you sow.

The Hindu doctrine of rebirth and karma was later elaborated and expanded by Buddha Sakyamuni, the founder of Buddhism. Buddha stated that it was important to act correctly and to live a pure and honest life. Only then could man free himself from the eternal cycle of life, death and being born again, the so-called wheel of rebirth. By acting correctly man could free himself from the karma of past lives, a condition for consciously returning to Nirvana or paradise, an eternal state of happiness.

At this point I wish to make a distinction between the concept of reincarnation and that of transmigration of the soul. Under the latter we might for example imagine a human soul being born into the body of an animal, something that certain Hindu factions believe to be possible. According to this view such a situation can occur when a person has developed in a lowly, 'animal', that is an 'ignoble', direction in a previous life. For reasons that will become clear later in my account, when I consider the difference between man and animal (see chapter 6), this view seems to me to be incorrect. In the context of this book the idea of reincarnation is only to be understood as *the continual rebirth of a human soul in a human body.* Incarnation is the descent of a human soul in a material body; reincarnation indicates that this occurs more than once, that the soul incarnates several (many) times in a material body with distinct periods of rest in between.

This immediately raises the question: what is the human soul? Naturally we are eager to know what it is that reincarnates.

A human being has many 'bodies'

Maybe you can best compare man in his entirety with an old-fashioned telescopic spyglass in which the various parts slide inside each other. Only the outer covering, the material body is visible. The other parts are 'inside'. For the sake of argument let us call the entire collection of innermost invisible coverings 'the soul'.

If we examine this image in more detail we see that the soul itself is again made up of various parts or 'bodies' that slide into each other like the spyglass. In literature on the subject the terms 'astral body', 'ethereal body' and 'spiritual body' are used for the individual components of the soul.

Everything in the material world surrounding us is organised, is arranged from large to small, coarse to fine, from simple to complicated. Is it not logical with regard to the body and soul to assume that there is also a certain order in the composition of man?

For example the constitutional states of solid, liquid and gas are known in the natural world. The solid state of any given substance is a condensation of the liquid state and the liquid state a condensation of the gaseous state.

The analogy does not stop here. We can view the soul as a collection of 'bodies' of different density or perhaps we should say: of different disposition? The analogy however is not a perfect match because ice, water and steam are all made up of the same molecules, of the same substance: H_2O. In view of their different names it seems to me that this is not the case for the various parts of the soul. Perhaps it is more appropriate to think in terms of different 'vibrational levels' or 'frequencies' or to think about the 'density of energy'. More about this later.

Thus the material body is the most 'condensed' covering of the soul.

Near-death

Maybe you are now asking yourself how you can know or experience that we have something like a soul, that we are more than just a physical body.

One indication for the fact that we are more than a mere physical body is the near-death-experience, a phenomenon which has received much attention over the last two decades. This experience in which the victim or patient has the feeling of being outside his body can occur after a serious accident or during an operation. From a distance he observes the doctors busily working with his heart and body while they try to reanimate him. The patient also has a very clear sense that he and his body are two completely different things.

It also sometimes happens that he or she sees a

rapidly moving 'film' in which the essential moments in his or her life are reviewed. People who have been through a near-death-experience sometimes experience other very beautiful things, and often have no desire to return to their earthly existence. Meetings with deceased family members and 'light entities' occur frequently. Afterwards life takes on a new meaning for many because of the profound experiences they have been through. Spiritual values become more important than material values, and people more important than money and possessions. An interesting aspect of the near-death-experience, pertaining especially to the credibility of such events, is that the reanimated patient can often recall precisely what people said or which medical procedures were carried out during the reanimation. To the great astonishment of the onlookers patients can sometimes give details about things (clothing for example) that would have been impossible for them to see from their position (for example on the operating table). Incidents have even been related that have occurred outside the reanimation room[2].

In addition, near-death-experiences occur all over the world and are thus not bound to a particular culture, religion or ideology. The books by Moody and Van Lommel which are mentioned in the bibliography cover these aspects in great detail.

I would however like to make the critical note that near-death-experiences that proceeded less pleasantly are seldom reported. The reports nearly always concern tranquil and loving meetings and experiences. I can also imagine that there are 'areas' in the non-material world which are not so pleasant to stay in during an out-of-body experience. When someone does talk about a near-death-experience, often a rather daunting act for many due to the anticipated dismissive reactions of an intolerant environment, it is usually the fine and the wonderful, and not the dreadful things that are initially trusted to the outsider.

Scientifically the various phenomena that appear during a near-death-experience have been attributed to hallucinations that are a consequence of reduced oxygen to the brain. Perhaps cerebral processes do play a part, but to assert that they account in full for the unusual experiences seems to me an unwarranted dismissal. They are so universal, and for the person involved so profound and often of such decisive significance for the rest of his life, that I cannot imagine that they are limited purely to the cerebral.

A sensation that is perhaps more familiar to most people than the near-death-experience just discussed, is the sensation that occurs just before we fall asleep in which the room around us gets larger and larger and we feel as though we are falling. In this respect sleep is known as 'the little death'. In the same way that the soul lets go of the body permanently in actual death, the link between body and soul becomes temporarily looser when we enter sleep. The soul 'drifts' outside the body, but still stays connected via a sort of umbilical cord, often described in the literature as the 'silver cord'.

In his books the American author Robert A. Monroe describes how he consciously leaves his body during sleep. This is known as 'astral projection'.

All these experiences indicate that people not only have a body but also know a state of existence that is possible without, or rather outside that body.

Incarnation

Summarising at this stage we arrive at the following image. Man consists of both an outermost material covering and an intangible component that we call the 'soul'.

The process of pairing, the 'sliding into each other' of the intangible soul and the material body, is called incarnation. How does this pairing come about?

In themselves both the process of incarnation and the preparation of the soul for this event are a great miracle. A superbly detailed account of this event from the spiritual point of view appears in the book *The Nine Months* by Anne and Daniel Meurois-Givaudan. Using clairvoyance the authors make contact with a soul that is preparing for a new life on earth. The account involves a woman called Rebecca who incarnates by a young married couple. We experience the entire pregnancy, incarnation and birth through the eyes of Rebecca.

The concrete linking of body and soul is a sort of 'magnetic' process in which the emissions of the body and the soul must be in perfect mutual correspondence. We could also express it like this: the 'frequency' of both parts must be exactly the same if a merging, a sliding into each other is to take place. In chemistry we find a comparable situation when, for example, two substances form a new bond only at a specific temperature, that is at a precise molecular frequency.

For various reasons a disturbance can arise during the linking manoeuvre between the body and the soul. An unsuccessful linking due to the foetus being physically insufficiently viable, may for example end in a miscarriage. An albeit successful although not so strong link could be an explanation for a condition such as epilepsy, in which 'the current occasionally fails' or 'the contact (between body and soul) is partially broken'.

An inadequate link between body and soul could sometimes play a role in mania too. For example, when a soul has such a weak emission that it is not properly connected to the body, another discarnate soul has the opportunity to make a connection with that same body. You then have the effect of a radio that is tuned in between two stations, where neither of the transmitters is clearly received or where one occasionally drowns out the other completely.

What we call human life is in fact the existence of successful pairings between body and soul. We live provided that the emissions from body and soul correspond to each other. If the emissions change this can bring about problems of such severity that the magnetism between body and soul is no longer strong enough to maintain the connection. This is the moment when death approaches.

Incarnation occurs about half way through the pregnancy. There are mothers who very consciously sense the moment at which the soul occupies the baby's body for the first time. This is often combined with the baby's first movements. At this point 'there also arises the peculiarly blissful feeling of the pregnant woman, in whom quite different intuitive perceptions set in from this moment: the awareness of the presence of the second spirit within her, the sensing of it.'[3] This does not however imply that no contact is possible between mother and child in the period preceding the actual incarnation. The connection between mother and child can date from previous incarnations for example, and some souls have possibly already chosen a particular set of parents long before there is mention of a pregnancy. Karmic factors play an important role here. I consider these in depth in chapter 2.

Dying

And then comes the inevitable departure from this earthly life, the moment when we have to say farewell to everyone and everything that is precious to us. Whatever we might believe, whatever conviction about life we might hold, we all view this moment with a certain trepidation. Most of us do not actually know what is (personally) awaiting us. And even the reports of those who have been through a near-death-experience do not expel our underlying anxiety.

Usually we are primarily afraid of dying itself, of having to give in to it, of losing control. What will we experience physically? Will it be coupled with pain, lack of oxygen or perhaps with a feeling of enlightenment and liberation? For man, dying is one of the most individual and thus possibly one of the most desolate experiences he ever faces.

I was present during the demise of my father. My girlfriend had withdrawn to the bedroom upstairs, my mother was asleep on the couch in the front room exhausted by all the emotions. I sat next to my father in a light conservatory. The doctor had told us that it would be over within a few hours. My father lay on his side with his back towards me and breathed heavily; he had pulmonary oedema. I had placed my hand on his back. In silence I asked him to let go, to leave. I quietly concentrated on this thought. Suddenly he gave a short jerk with his head. Soon afterwards my girlfriend came downstairs and told me that she had sensed a sort of light, a feeling of liberation. This was the moment for me that my father passed over ...

Where are we between two lives?

We are in the beyond. The magnetic connection between the soul and the physical sheath is broken. The body will now be returned to the earth by the next of kin or transformed into ash by the flames. The soul will continue its journey.

Between two earthly lives, man (the soul) resides in the beyond, in the ethereal sphere. There, in conformity with our telescopic model, his ethereal body constitutes his outermost covering and he perceives using his ethereal senses. Whilst residing in the beyond he goes through many experiences similar to that of an earthly life, only now with the difference that he finds himself in an environment that is completely in accordance with his inner nature and maturity. It is different on earth. Here we come into contact with people of diverse 'spiritual' plumage and are thus able to 'learn' both more and faster albeit in an agreeable or a less agreeable sense. The purpose of the phase in between two lives is for man to be seriously confronted with his inner self, in a manner impossible on earth. It thus provides an opportunity for man to mature and realise his imperfections.

Another reason for his stay in the beyond is for him to undergo a releasing and healing process related to the things that he experienced in his previous life. Furthermore he must prepare himself for his next stay in the material world.

We have a chance to regenerate in this other world, particularly if we were ill or had a difficult old age in the previous life, but also from the many psychic wounds (traumata) inflicted upon us.

It seems that some souls cannot let go of a particular life situation, so much so that they do not even realise that they have moved on to the 'other world'. Such cases are described by the Japanese esoterist and clairvoyant Dr Hiroshi Motoyama in his book *Karma and Reincarnation*. He describes the remarkable case of a chieftain who lived 3,500 years ago and who has stayed in, what he calls, the astral dimension since that time: 'This tribal leader and his people continue to live in the deep past. Their world is thickly wooded. Wild dogs run freely. They live in small villages, make their own pottery, reside in neolithic style structures. The chieftain of this tribe still lives a luxurious life, pampered by his many wives. All this is going on in the astral dimension at the same time and in the same place that we are living out our modern lives in the physical dimension. I have been able to make some contact with this entity and he has come to have some understanding of the way in which the world has changed, but he is happy with his ancient ways and does not wish to change anything.

He is just one example of someone who is satisfied to be existing in a dimension where thoughts create reality. People in similarly contented situations may choose to stay that way for hundreds, even thousands of years.'[4]

The last sentence of this quote is of particular interest. According to Motoyama we 'create' the ethereal reality, that we re-enter after discarding our physical body, with our thoughts and feelings. A second point raised here is that we can apparently decide to continue with a particular situation in the beyond. However the question remains: is there such a thing as a conscious choice or a real decision at this level? Later we will consider the law of attraction of homogeneous species, commonly known as the 'like seeks like' principle. According to this principle we remain attached to that with which we are linked, be it a person, a place or a particular life situation, via a strong connection that we developed during our life on earth. Thus this seems to be more an issue of overwhelming dependency, or a leaning towards, rather than one of free choice.

Different lives, other circumstances

In the above we discussed the descent of the soul of man into his body. If this event takes place often, in other words when this process repeats itself through time, or in different historical periods, we can speak of reincarnation. Each time the soul incarnates in another body, that is in a different (or possibly the same) mother. Thus the same soul acquires a different form, another cloak, because it is born to other parents. The earthly circumstances are also different each time. Even the sex can differ. You can incarnate as a woman in the next life, even though you were a man in the previous one, and vice versa.

The why and the wherefore of such differences will

become clearer when we consider the concept of karma in the next chapter.

How often do we return?

The question is often asked if this process of reincarnation goes on without end, if we incarnate endlessly on earth. The answers given to this question vary. Certain spiritual groups and religions express the view that it is undeniably useful and desirable to escape from the so-called cycle of rebirth in the long run, but that in principle it never has to end. Thus that the possibility for reincarnation remains present for many years to come.

I hold the opinion that we are on earth, in the material, in order to develop and to 'improve' (spiritually) and that we do not have unlimited time to do this. The earth, just like everything else material, moves through a specific development with periods of generation, ripening and decay and certainly does not have eternal life. At a certain stage in the development of the earth this could mean that souls, most of whom have incarnated on earth many times before, no longer have enough time to develop themselves further. It seems a logical idea that at a certain stage in the development of the earth no more 'new' souls can incarnate on earth.[5] 'New' souls are souls that descend for the first time into a material body. We can of course also consider the possibility of incarnating on other planets in entirely different solar systems with perhaps similar conditions to those on earth. There is such an inconceivable number of solar systems in our known universe that this possibility cannot be dismissed.

Is it not more obvious to assume that the soul is allotted a specific time to develop itself, just like everything else in this transient material world, and that thereafter it is no longer able to incarnate on this material plane, but has to develop further in intangible worlds?

Time can appear terribly long here when measured against human earthly standards, although actually when viewed cosmically a couple of million years is relatively short.

We come across parallels of the processes described above in the natural world. Here everything happens in its own time too: one sort of plant flowers in spring, another in summer and a third in autumn. One common requirement of these plants is however that the seeds, which need a certain amount of time to develop into a plant, are in (are put into) the ground a little time beforehand. The seeds in turn are only able to germinate during a certain period and under specific conditions. For example they need a frosty night or a certain amount of moisture or warmth.

All natural processes follow a similar course; one stage follows another; the sequence of events is usually irreversible. A germ grows, flowers, ripens and then disintegrates into substances that in their turn form the matter from which new germs originate. This does not only happen on a small scale. Larger cosmic processes, up to and including the creation and destruction of solar systems, also proceed according to these 'laws'.

In conclusion it does not seem illogical to me to assume that human existence, on both a large and small scale, is subjected to the same rhythms and cycles as those which I have described above.

What is time?

It may be fruitful to take a closer look at the concept of time since we have referred to it several times.

When we think about 'time', most of us see a chain of events that take place one after the other. We see a line and on it a point representing the present. The past lies behind this point and the future stretches away in front of it. Time is a clock ticking away, minute after minute, hour after hour.

Yet we all know the feeling of time apparently passing more quickly when we are enjoying ourselves or are completely engrossed in something. On the other hand everyone also knows how long five short minutes can appear, for example when we are waiting for something, are bored or find ourselves in an emergency situation.

Thus here we are dealing with another sort of time, a 'subjective' time, that is dependent on something within us, on the way in which we experience the reality around us.

We also develop problems with time at incredibly high speeds and over extremely long distances. For example, after a space journey lasting thirty (earth) years, we are only one year older.

It is not my intention to give a conclusive account of time here. I wish only to indicate that the concept of time is not equivalent to the seconds and minutes on the alarm clock by our bed.

People who have had a near-death-experience for example, have seen their whole life flash past them in a fraction of a second. The entire near-death-experience, in which they go through a great deal, lasts perhaps a few minutes.

Furthermore, scientists investigating sleep have shown that we move our eyes very quickly during certain dream phases (known as rapid eye movements). It appears that events happen so quickly in dreams that our eyes can hardly keep up.

If we accept that our perception of time is dependent on our inner state, we can draw a parallel between our subjective sense of time during the day and the feeling that we have when we dream and during near-death-experiences. In all three situations we experience a great deal, although the 'earthly' time in minutes and hours is extremely short. All three occurrences have in common that 'something' within us is very intensely experiencing, undergoing and involved in something, and that this appears to 'dislocate' the concept of time that we usually employ.

It appears that there are two types of time: one for our intellect and one for our heart or soul. One is neatly measured with a device called a clock. The other eludes objectivity because no two people are identical and everyone experiences things differently within.

Perhaps we can speak of a time that is coupled to matter, to the material, and of a time that is 'valid' in the intangible part of creation.

It appears as if perception of time is related to the density or nature of the world in which we find ourselves, as though we experience less in material reality than in ethereal reality during the same earthly time period. It appears as if life in the beyond is much richer and more intense than in the material world.

Would it be correct to suppose that in our experience time passes faster as the 'sphere' in which the observer finds himself becomes rarer, less dense? Can we perhaps see a parallel between the division of man into various 'bodies', as presented above, and the composition of the universe, that is both the material, visible part and the intangible part that is invisible to the physical eye? In turn, does the non-material part of the universe also consist of different 'spheres' of varying density, each with a 'different' time?

Little by little we have arrived at a considerably more differentiated and relative notion of time and have been able to establish that the notion of time with which we started, is actually linked to our physical state, to being in a body. Other concepts of time and space apply outside the body.

Man: a microcosm

It seems to me worthwhile to retain the image of a 'universe' consisting of spheres and man consisting of various 'bodies'. It appears that man is a kind of reflection of the division of the universe, that he contains all the qualities or densities which determine the different 'spheres' in the universe.

If we use a metaphor, we see a human germ adopting different coverings during its journey through the spheres and finally, as a complete soul, pulling on a physical cloak as it reaches the physical world for its first incarnation. Additionally we might suppose that all these bodies are equipped with senses, just like our physical body, and that they are just as capable of perceiving in the sphere to which they correspond as we are here on earth with our physical senses.

If we take as a starting point that the various bodies of man in fact refer to different states of aggregation or energy density or, put another way, to different vibrations, it would mean that we should be able to perceive two 'realities'. That is, in addition to our physical world we should also be able to perceive a world with a higher frequency, a world in which, as we have already seen, a different time applies.

Indeed it is thanks to the multiple layers of his being that man is sometimes permitted to cast a glance into 'another' dimension and is able to see relationships between events that are invisible to the physical eye.

Why do we know little or nothing about our 'past lives'?

A question that is often asked when you talk to people about reincarnation is: 'If I have lived so many times before, why can't I remember anything about it?' You could answer this question with a counter-question: 'Seen from a higher perspective does it really make sense for you to know anything about your past lives? Isn't it simply curiosity that would be motivating you? Isn't it far better to start a new life with a blank consciousness, so that you can *spontaneously* pay off possible (karmic) debts and collect outstanding (karmic) claims?' I imagine that if it is necessary to know something about a past life, you will know it intuitively one way or the other. Perhaps not always as a conscious image accessible to the mind, but as an inner realisation as to why you have to go through something, when something happens to you.

We would probably waste much time on all sorts of 'interesting' details from a past life, time that we desperately need to work on our inner perfection and for experiencing the here and now. This is why it is beneficial that there is a shield, albeit sometimes very thin, between our present existence and that which went before. Do we not already have enough difficulty letting go of things from our immediate past, or trying to meet those who have caused us grief in this life with an open and forgiving mind?

Imagine for once that you could see precisely what type of relationship you had had with everyone you come across in your life. I think there would be no question of spontaneously making amends or getting something back. If we also remember that we were often in a reverse relationship in a previous life (for example parent-child/child-parent), conscious knowledge of this would make the burden too heavy, and the specific lesson would maybe never be learnt.

Can reincarnation be proved?

The word 'evidence' was used in the introduction. In the scientific sense there is no real hard evidence of reincarnation. However in the course of the twentieth century many very intriguing facts have emerged that make reincarnation more acceptable to the sceptic.

Prophet in spite of himself

One of the people who made a major contribution towards popularising the reincarnation idea was the American Edgar Cayce. As a child, born in 1877 in Hopkinsville, Kentucky, he already showed unusual perceptive abilities. At the age of six he told his parents that he had conversations with recently deceased family members during a sort of 'vision'. He could also fall asleep on his school books and then awaken with a 'photographic impression' of the contents of the book. He even knew precisely on which page a certain passage could be found!

At the age of twenty-one the muscles in his throat became paralysed and he lost his voice. When the doctors could find no physical cause for his illness, Cayce asked a friend to help him evoke the state of consciousness again with which he had learnt his lessons as a child. He went into a sort of trance and then told in a clear and distinct voice what needed to be done in order to get rid of his ailment. Later it became obvious that, in trance, Cayce could give very exact and effective information about the health problems of people who turned to him for help. He often prescribed unorthodox remedies for the complaints. Cayce, who came from an orthodox Christian background, did not initially want to know about the idea of reincarnation. Later in his trance sessions he indicated that certain of his clients' problems were associated with links from past lives and deeds. When Cayce died in 1945 he left behind 14,000 stenographic reports of trance sessions with more than 6,000 different people, many including references to past lives.[6]

I find the Cayce story especially convincing because Cayce was a very devout and upright man, averse to any tendency towards occultism and esotericism.

Reincarnation research
Additional pioneering work in the area of reincarnation has been performed by Professor Dr Ian Stevenson. In

his sensational book *Twenty Cases Suggestive of Reincarnation* he gives detailed accounts of his investigation of interesting cases of small children in India who can remember many details from past lives. He provides a meticulous report of the verification of all the details from the original setting of their past life. All the children appeared, given the accuracy of the reincarnation hypothesis, to have incarnated anew within a couple of years, so that the information that they gave could still be checked.

One of the cases that was closely examined by Stevenson is that of the boy Prakash. In April 1950, a ten-year-old boy named Nirmal died in his parents' house in Kosi Kalan, a town in the district of Mathura in the Indian province of Uttar Pradesh. He was the son of the merchant Sri Bholanath Jain.

In August 1951 the wife of Sri Brijlal Varshnay in Chatta delivered a son, whom they named Prakash. When he was four and a half years old, he woke in the middle of the night and ran out of the house. When he was restrained he said that he 'belonged' in Kosi Kalan, that he was called Nirmal and that he wanted to return to his old house. He said that his father was called Bholanath. This happened several times.

In 1956, when he was about five years old, he reproduced the names of Nirmal's family members and friends. However, he had forgotten these again five years later. His family tried everything to get him to forget his past life. In 1961 he came in contact with Sri Bholanath for the first time and immediately recognised him as 'father'.

Stevenson interviewed a large number of people from both families plus a few outside observers.

Practically all the reports showed that Prakash pos-
sessed a very detailed knowledge of people and things.
The family of Sri Bholanath was completely convinced
that their deceased Nirmal was born again.

Stevenson comments that it is extraordinarily
difficult to explain this case using telepathy. The recognition of people, the reproduction of their names,
occupations and habits was startling. That Prakash
failed to recognise daughter Memo, who was born after
Nirmal's death, and confused her with someone else
was striking.[7]

Back to 'earlier lives'

A third source, and in the eyes of the sceptic perhaps
the least credible, is regression or reincarnation therapy.
Therapists in this field describe numerous cases of
clients being liberated from a particular problem that
had been troubling them for years, after a regression
to an 'earlier life'. Often the client concerned had to
re-experience the circumstances and the incident which
had led to his current problem. By doing so an episode
could be rounded off and the incident in question
would no longer have a traumatic effect in the here and
now. According to reincarnation therapists, phobias,
fear of fire, water and small or dark places in particular
often have their roots in ghastly events from earlier
lives. There is however something to be said against the
link between psychic problems and earlier lives. For
some therapists reincarnation is a sort of 'working
hypothesis' rather than a reality; it is most important
to them that the therapy is effective and that the patient
gets rid of his phobia. We could also raise questions

about the method of regression therapy itself, in which forms of hypnosis are sometimes used (not in all cases). Taking into account the fact that you expose the patient to great risks during hypnosis, something which I do not intend to discuss in this book, I ask myself if poking around in earlier lives is such a beneficial thing. I have touched upon this subject earlier (see page 23).

In conclusion I would like to state that I find Edgar Cayce's trance sessions and Professor Stevenson's minutely documented case histories especially convincing as 'evidence' in favour of reincarnation. They provide a coherent and logical view and are in many ways verifiable, certainly with regard to Stevenson's cases. This is why they must not be excluded in a book such as this. However, we will come across far more persuasive arguments for the reality of reincarnation in the following chapters on karma.

−2−

KARMA

Many people ask the question why. Often they do not understand what happens to them. Why me? Why must this happen to me now? Or when it concerns something marvellous or beautiful: what have I done to deserve this? Evidently a feeling of injustice arises in many people, and there is a need to understand, to see a logic behind 'blind coincidence'.

Karma: life and movement

In the text above we have developed a fairly static view of the composition of man and the cosmos. In this chapter we will now see that everything springs into life and action when the idea of karma is introduced. In Sanskrit the word 'karma' means 'work' or 'to act'. Our actions however have certain consequences; this is not only a psychological mechanism, but also a sort of 'natural law'. Our actions set the entire machinery, the entire radar equipment of our existence into motion. Under 'action' we should understand not only our concrete deeds, such as going to the baker to buy bread, but also our thoughts and words. We can perhaps imagine that our words have certain consequences. We all know what words can do. But our thoughts? Do they have a particular influence too? And I am not just referring to the effects at the perceptible and physical level, but also to the silent influence that our thoughts have on the people around us or even on those far away. Do our thoughts also pertain to our 'actions', our karma?

Law of energy conservation

The law of energy conservation is familiar to the physical sciences. If we put energy into something, that energy comes out again. Furthermore the total amount of energy in a system remains constant provided that we do not add or subtract energy from it.

For example when we use muscle power during cycling, a portion of the energy is converted into moving the bicycle; a portion disappears as warmth due to friction with the road. The total amount of energy that we put into the activity is however equal to the sum of the different sorts of energy resulting from our activity.

Likewise we can view karma as a sort of energy that we produce with our thoughts, words, and deeds. Karmic 'energy' no more disappears than the quantifiable physical energy which we were just discussing. Karmic energy also remains stored 'somewhere'. We might ask ourselves what happens to karmic energy.

Let us return briefly again to the physical sciences and to the law of 'action = reaction'. A ball that we throw against a wall comes back to us with the same energy = speed (minus the energy that dispersed as warmth). We find a component of the great karmic law here, the law of reciprocal action.

Reciprocal action: a principle of life

The natural world around us is actually a grand example of the principle of reciprocal action and we can learn a great deal from it. All parts of nature (as a living system) form a sort of network, related to each other and mutually reacting to each other. Our body for example is a system in which all sorts of reciprocal actions take place. Furthermore we know of ecosystems in which animals, plants and climate influence each other strongly.

The principle of reciprocal action is essential to the maintenance of life; through it a sort of balance is achieved. It is now evident that all sorts of natural living systems are looking for balance, a harmony that they will possibly never attain. Striving to reach such a state is nevertheless a fundamental mechanism of all life.

Expressed in more human terms 'reciprocal action' can also be described as 'giving and taking'.

Psychologically speaking most of us tend towards situations where giving and taking are in balance. Many people feel awkward when this is not the case. Does the unconscious desire for balance also play a role here?

Cosmic balance

Perhaps we should regard the axiom that karma, once accrued, always requires settlement (in favourable or unfavourable form) as the striving of a much larger mechanism than ourselves for balance in the cosmic sense.

We can produce various concrete examples, and each time the principle of a system seeking balance reappears.

Seen purely objectively, the energy that comes our way in the form of an incident may be a retroaction, a deed to restore balance.

If we adopt this point of view for everything that happens to us, that a retroaction is an attempt to restore balance, to correct a certain partiality, then entirely new perspectives open up. We can ask ourselves at what point or at which moment in our existence we became 'unbalanced'. Intuitively we often know this only too well although we might have difficulty accepting it and have perhaps hidden it 'out of sight' of our conscience. We could view difficulties as possibilities, fate as a chance. If we look at illness in this light for example, it can perhaps show us the way to a life that we had forgotten to live, to the 'hidden agenda' of the unconscious, to things that we had not yet 'digested' and still need to work on. When we consider the theme 'love, truth and justice' (chapter 5) this aspect of karmic law will be discussed in yet more detail.

The way karma works

In the introduction I indicated that I assume the existence of an ethereal world 'outside' visible material reality. It seems to me that the relationship between these two 'realities' plays an important role in the questions: what precisely is karma and how does it work?

We cannot simply make connections between things that we see around us in the one reality and processes that occur in the other invisible reality. It is for this very reason that many people find it so difficult to accept the idea of karma as real. How for instance can you see the link between event x and a possible retroaction or reciprocal action y if they are separated from each other by time and space?

If something is to remain of a thought, word or action in a non-material reality, where it will wait for us before returning to the material world, then analogous to the law of energy conservation just stated, an ethereal energetic antagonist must be formed in the ethereal world in addition to gross material energy.

This is now exactly what certain people gifted with clairvoyance see happening. An action gives rise to a certain energy in the beyond. This energy remains connected to the person in question and in its own time returns to its point of origin, according to the principle of reciprocal action, and takes on a concrete form in his life, or if we believe in reincarnation in a later life. Thoughts also have a specific energy and adopt a specific ethereal form and remain connected to their point of origin too. The idea that we can think what we want to think without bearing any responsibility for our thoughts appears not to be in agreement with the laws of the cosmos.

Is everything that happens to us karma?

Have you only yourself to blame for all the troubles (or all the good things) that happen to you? This question is often asked when the conversation turns to karma. Some people just cannot imagine that 'innocents' have to put up with so much misery.

If we view karma as retroaction for a word, thought or action that we once brought into the world, in this earthly life or another, then we will encounter that retroaction in one way or another. However, this does not imply that we once personally caused everything that now happens to us, or that karma is only to be seen as the fruits of our past activities. Perhaps we sometimes need a certain experience in order to develop further, or we have 'dozed off' on our life path and need to be shaken awake in order not to 'lose control of the wheel' and 'miss the path'. I would not call this karma but a (well-intended) nudge of fate.

It is possible that a phenomenon referred to in the literature as 'spiritual guidance' or 'spiritual companion' might also play a role here. This spiritual companion or 'guide' as he is sometimes called, is a soul that has passed to the beyond and has taken the task upon himself to help another soul who still remains on earth. This entity, it may be male or female, must not differ too much in spiritual maturity from the person whom he guides; otherwise he is unable to bring about essential contact. He or she is usually just a little further in his or her development, still close enough to understand the other and just developed enough to be able to oversee the problems of the earthly person from a 'higher point of view'. The person on earth can be stimulated and inspired by his guide in that he receives precisely the stimulus that he needs to move on again and to grow further. It goes without saying that such 'warnings' can in turn also be a reason why something happens to us that could have been prevented if we had only 'listened'.

Another more or less connected reason for the unpleasant things that happen to us can be summarised under the notion of 'lack of vigilance'. Vigilance plays an important role in nature. For example an animal that loses guard for a few seconds easily falls prey to a predator. Vigilance is a very valuable quality for humans too. By this I do not mean an attitude of distrust and suspicion towards others but rather a lively mind, a well developed intuition, with which we can 'feel in our bones' that something or someone is no good.

The story goes that in times gone by when people lived closer to nature, they were better able to predict natural disasters. Apart from the possibility that they were warned by nature beings, who were invisible to most people (see page 83), it seems that at that time people were also very aware of the movements of animals. A significant and sudden migration of animals at an unexpected time (for example birds or small rodents) could be the forewarning of an earthquake.

Karma, in the sense of retroaction from a past life, does not have to be the only reason why something happens to us. In addition to living further and further from nature, we have allowed our sensitivity or intuition more or less to wither away by placing too much emphasis on our intellect. By doing so we have lost the ability to experience this sort of thing.

An innocent person who is unjustly harmed by another, and not because he ever did anything of the sort to anyone himself, can make spiritual progress because of it. You could compare this to a man who denies himself full pleasure in life right now by putting his money into a savings account so that he can live without money worries later. The 'sacrifice' that is made now bears sweet fruits later. It does however depend on how the 'victim' deals with the injustice that is done to him. If for instance he becomes seriously embittered or traumatised by it, then this can continue to trouble him past the boundaries of his current life. If he becomes wiser and spiritually more mature from the episode and is able to inwardly forgive his 'enemies', then it is a spiritual gain. There are people, Corrie ten Boom for example, who are so convinced of the power of love and the senselessness of hate, that they have eventually been able to forgive their concentration camp torturers.[1]

Of course the one who caused the misery remains completely outside this process. In principle he must reap what *he* has sown in the world.

Karma and charity

The idea of charity, of 'loving your neighbour', is still an important issue in our culture, strongly influenced as it has been by Christian thought. Luckily people are still prepared to help their fellow creatures, be they far away or near by, as witnessed in relief operations or normal everyday kindness to a colleague or neighbour. Is charity still meaningful from the karmic point of view? How should we relate to the other and to his karma, for which he is ultimately responsible, and which he has to resolve himself?

We must always help, wherever and whenever possible. Why? In the first place it is not our duty to 'judge' the activities of other people. We are not in a position to judge what it is someone has to resolve. Besides we have just seen how complicated the background to someone's situation can be. And even though we might be able to take a look behind the screens, it is still not up to us to draw conclusions from this. Besides we have enough to do with our own parcel of assignments. We have to get on with sorting that out!

Moreover, it is precisely in this sort of situation that the possibility arises to give, to interact, and by doing so to resolve our own karma.

The best contacts, the finest friendships often develop in a situation in which you can really mean something to someone, in a material or a spiritual sense.

Karmic factors in reincarnation

Why do we reincarnate in this land or among this folk? Why do we find ourselves in these circumstances or with these parents? In light of the foregoing it seems obvious to suppose that karmic influences also play an important role here. Seeing that no-one now incarnates on earth for the first time, something that I explained earlier (see page 18), every soul must have certain karmic links from previous lives.

A karmic link is the result of close contact between two souls in this life or in an earlier life. Seeing the many different forms a relationship can take and the endless variation in intensity, we can be sure as individuals that we have many karmic links with other people. We can include family, friends, colleagues, violent confrontations, etc. We are in a kind of network with all sorts of lines running to different people and times.

Apart from possible karmic relationships another mechanism also plays a role in the question by whom, where and under which circumstances we incarnate. This factor is the principle of attraction of homogeneous species. We discuss this in more depth when we consider the laws of creation.

Parents and children

When I put my daughter to bed I sometimes just sit beside her before I say goodnight and go downstairs. I listen to the babbling of her voice and occasionally drift away with my own thoughts and musings. Sometimes feelings of gratitude wash over me, that we as parents are trusted with the responsibility of letting this beautiful little person grow up into a healthy young woman, that in the years she has been with us she has had the chance to make a good start in the world and to develop her talents. I realise time and again that it is a great privilege to be a parent.

And the miracle only gets bigger when you stop to think that essentially you have, in a spiritual sense, a 'grown up' soul in your care, whom you sometimes suspect to be wiser than yourself, from whom you have something to learn, perhaps even an 'old' friend. It is possible that there are old ties. Later when she is older and goes her own way or perhaps at the end of your earthly life you will maybe understand the impact her arrival had on you, what a help she was to you (in a spiritual sense).

When we look at relations between parents and children from the karma and reincarnation perspective, many things that play a role in such a relationship take on new significance. Of course the young child is not able to experience this consciously. However, a parent can ask himself to what extent karmic relations or attraction of homogeneous species play a part in the difficult relationship with the child, particularly in special cases where the parent perceives the child as troublesome. It is in this way that the child can act as our mirror. In principle the latter applies to all our relations whether problem-free or troubled.

I believe that every parent-child relation has a deep significance for *both* participants and that the relationship brings with it the things we need for our inner development, although these things are not always pleasant. It is indeed the people with whom we live closely for a while that help us to mature.

Furthermore, as parents we naturally have an enormous responsibility for our children. What we are to them and what we give to them is fairly determinant for the rest of their lives and from the karmic perspective can have great consequences for both us and the child.

There is a wonderful passage about this subject in the 'Grail Message': 'The causes working to determine the conditions into which a soul is born often lie far back, just as they determine the period under the influences of which the child will enter the physical world, so that during its earthly pilgrimage these conditions may continually influence it and achieve what this particular soul needs for its redemption, moulding, casting off karma, and further development.

But this does not happen in a one-sided manner for the child only, but the threads spin on automatically so that the reciprocal action is also felt in the earthly surroundings.

The parents give the child just what it needs for its further development, just as vice versa the child gives to its parents, be it good or evil. For further development and advancement it is of course necessary in this connection to become free from an evil by personally experiencing it, whereby it will be recognised for what it is and cast off. It is the reciprocal action which always brings about the opportunity for this. Without the operation of this law man could never become really free from anything that has happened to him.'2

Karma and free will

Surely the idea of karma opposes the notion of free will? Doesn't having karma necessarily imply a sort of predestined existence and thus an enormous restriction to your possibilities? Initially it might seem so, all the more so because we Westerners often associate the idea of karma with the (prejudiced?) image of the fatalistic, submissive attitude of the Oriental.

Of course there is an element of truth in the notion that karma restricts our possibilities, although as I have already indicated, we can also see restrictions or obstacles as possibilities, as assignments: karma as chance!

Nonetheless my opinion remains that we *are free in our choice* at every moment. This is our 'freedom' and also our responsibility. If we accept this we can acknowledge that we are partly determined by our past, by our 'prehistory' from this and earlier lives.

The question is only *how* determining it is, how strongly we are attached to it, how limited we have become because of it. Are we perhaps trapped in it? And how can we become free from it again?

If we think back to the image in the first chapter of the germ that incarnated on earth as a person for the first time in its cosmic existence, we can perhaps feel what it is like not to have karma. We can also think of a child or adolescent taking its first steps in the world. Still 'innocent', open to everything, prepared to fall and get up again. Further driven by a strong desire to experience the world, to smell and taste everything. In this way we collect karma, become connected to the world, to other souls on earth; perhaps we also become tied and tangled by attachments and strong tendencies, do things in which we burden ourselves with karma. And here we are then, now, in this life, in a situation and with a personality that is actually the result of our entire existence up to this point.

If we think back through all the experiences and layers in ourselves to the original spirit (germ), we find our essential, undamaged self, and perhaps realise how much excess ballast we carry around with us, impurities that we really do not want but that have crept in when we were not sufficiently alert.

How can we cast off this ballast, ascend freely to 'lighter heights' and be truly free? The answer is just as simple as the question. We can only neutralise the karma that we bring with us from a previous life by changing our inner attitude in such a way that we do not, in the first place, form any more new adverse karma and secondly by paying off old karmic debts. The concrete possibilities for doing this will most certainly arise if we are open to them. This brings the dissolution and resolution of karma into the here and now, the moment in which I write these words and the instant in which you read them.

With this we have actually already said what free will is, namely the possibility of making a choice here and now. Only with this realisation are we truly able to create freedom for ourselves and to put a stop to the chain of unfavourable karmic retroaction. We really do have our fate in our own hands. But this is only the first most important step. Time and again we will come into contact with old retroaction which brings perhaps less pleasant experiences with it. And yet we will have the feeling of slowly making headway, of climbing 'higher' with every step.

In closing this chapter on karma I would like to say one more thing. When you chop the chips will fly, meaning that in our attempt to free ourselves of karma, we must be prepared to deal with the confrontation life brings. Some people who walk the spiritual path cannot resist the temptation to 'cultivate' their newly acquired belief and to partially withdraw from the 'bad' world outside or at least to do this in thought and attitude. It seems to me that it is actually our task to deal totally with whatever confronts us and to fully experience and go through everything that comes our way. We will without doubt make 'mistakes' and 'blunders' but this is always better than not making choices through not acting or avoiding taking responsibility. I am convinced that whatever comes our way is always in agreement with our actual, inner abilities, many of which we are probably not even aware of.

In the long run it is only intended to help us further. When we can accept this with confidence, we find the space and freedom in ourselves to look at the situation closely and to understand the lesson. This seems to me to be the comforting wisdom of this beautiful world.

–3–

KARMA IN HISTORICAL PERSPECTIVE

We live in a world full of tension and conflict. Millions of people worldwide are on the run; in more than a hundred countries local conflicts of varying severity continue to rage. Millions of the approximately 6 billion earth inhabitants suffer hunger, are poorly fed or housed and lack the most basic essentials of existence. In the meantime earthquakes, droughts, forest fires and other 'natural disasters', which are often partially due to the interference of man, seem to be increasing in number – not to mention worldwide environmental pollution, escalating violence and constantly increasing criminality. Unfortunately eighty per cent of the news on TV, radio and in the papers is 'bad news'. However much governments, organisations or individuals do their best to relieve the distress, to turn the tide or offer assistance, it seems like water off a duck's back. Such gigantic processes have been set in motion that it would take the collective effort of the entire population to alter the direction or bring a halt to the current development. In any case this effort should be many times greater than that with which we now console ourselves on both a spiritual and material level.

Let us attempt to see how we can understand the background to the present state of the world from a spiritual point of view. In my opinion something has gone wrong with the development of man, particularly at the spiritual level.

Key concepts in our inquiry will again be the words 'karma' and 'reciprocal action'. Concepts with which we can better understand the mechanism behind the reality of this time. We shall also consider the question why it is that such an enormous accumulation of events is happening right now. Are we perhaps in a transitional phase or at an important turning point?

The boomerang of fate and karma

'Man shall reap what he sows'. The functioning of the cosmos is actually indicated by these familiar words from the Bible (Galatians 6:7). When we look in more detail at the image with respect to nature, we see that when we sow one grain of wheat, we get thirty grains in return. Furthermore a wheat germ does not yield an ear of rye, and rye in turn does not produce oats. Applied to human actions this means that we always get back what we have put into the world and that it comes back *multiplied*. It is a sort of boomerang which confronts us all sooner or later, in a pleasant or unpleasant form.

As already stated, that which comes our way (in life) is called our karma or fate. It is good to know that we can never blame another for what happens to us, that we are primarily responsible ourselves. Also, as

mentioned earlier, it is not only our actions that determine karma; our thoughts and words are also 'energy'
and have their effect on what happens to us later.

Thoughts are forces

In the last chapter brief mention was made of homogeneous nature. Well, just as like-minded people are
attracted to each other in everyday life, similar
thoughts and feelings are attracted to each other too.
These form force fields in the beyond that in turn are
capable of influencing people who are open to thoughts
or feelings of the same nature. Thus we can imagine
immense force fields of love existing at the ethereal
level that are constantly being fed and strengthened by
thoughts and feelings of love. Likewise areas of hate
and depression also exist, fuelled by those in great
misery, those experiencing multiple problems or those
harbouring intense feelings of hatred.

A concrete example close to home which highlights
this was the bloody ethnic conflicts in former Yugoslavia.
Can you imagine the thought and emotional energies
that were released? First the political leaders worked on
the nationalistic feelings of the different population
groups and the already prominent force fields corresponding to these sentiments were fuelled. Perhaps we
can ask ourselves how our own thoughts and feelings of
unease and aggression contributed to the strengthening
of this sort of force field. What happens in former
Yugoslavia is perhaps not so far removed from our own
view of the world as we would like it to be. We could
give shape to this 'involvement' in a positive way by
impartially thinking of the people there with countless

thoughts of light and love, instead of becoming upset, powerlessly angry about this sort of affair and further strengthening the fields of revenge and hatred.

Individual versus collective karma

In chapter 2 we have already given extensive consideration to the subject of karma, in the first instance considering individuals and what happened to them. We have also stated that man as an individual is responsible for his words, thoughts and actions. Although we cannot perceive words and thoughts in a concrete way, viewed energetically they will have their retroaction in later life, immediately or in the future.

Individuals however join together in groups or are part of a people or a tribe. As a unit such a group can also act and thus also create karma that must be repaid or returned to them as a blessing.

Let us look at a concrete example. What the German machine of destruction did to the Jews before and during the Second World War can be viewed as a collective karma of the German people, that in one way or another has to be neutralised. I do not believe that we as human beings can oversee how such a process takes place. Here too repayment can take place at different levels, from concrete financial reparations and compensations to the heroic and courageous stance of the German people in relation to helping refugees, the Third World, etcetera.

When we remember that the German people have also been given a great deal, we only have to name Luther, Bach, Goethe, Beethoven and many other great artists and philosophers, it is particularly poignant to see how they broke with this trend. Further we can also recall that it was these very people who wanted to drive another spiritually gifted people, the Jews, to destruction.

A comparison between the fate of the Jews and the German people springs to mind in another sense too. When Moses brought the Ten Commandments to the Jews on Mount Sinai they had made the Golden Calf at the suggestion of Moses' brother Aaron. As a punishment they had to wander in the desert for forty years in sight of the Promised Land. They had placed matter above spirit.

Germany was pierced in the heart with the fall of the 'thousand-year-old' Third Reich and isolated for a period of forty years by a wall of barbed wire and concrete (and worse). Had the Germans not failed to recognise their spiritual calling? Had they not also placed the Golden Calf of material prosperity that Hitler held before them above the message from the Light that one of them delivered to them, *nota bene* in their own language and in their own time? Had they not misused their spiritual potential, with which they were so richly endowed and with which they could have enriched the world, for the wrong purpose? And of all people it was the Jews who got the blame for all of their problems and became the victims of the erroneous direction which they had taken.

National karma

The previously mentioned Japanese researcher Dr Hiroshi Motoyama examines the concept of national karma.[1] He writes: 'But when I look at Japan using non-physical perception, I see a very different picture.

48

Karma in
Historical
Perspective

Rather than mountains and rivers, I see a vast underlying Spirit. (...) Each nation on earth has its own
Spirit, and that Spirit has its own karma. (...) The
karma of the National Spirit affects everyone living in
the country, whether they are born there or immigrate
from other places.

During normal times,' Dr Motoyama continues,
'we are free to act out our individual karmic dramas
while living on any given national soil. In states of
national emergency such as wartime, however, most
individuals become powerless before the state as ants
before an oncoming steamroller. This is true of any
situation in which a large proportion of the populace
meets with death at the same time: war, famine,
plague, and is due to the fact, simply, that the National
Spirit is incomparably larger than that of an individual
human being. Most people, therefore, become subsumed
in any major manifestation of national karma occurring around them.'

Thus far Motoyama, who supposes in his description that a people have a sort of collective spiritual
identity that transcends the individual and as such can
create its own karma. How come that all these individuals form precisely this specific people? Again we can
perceive the effect of the power of attraction of the
homogeneous. Souls that incarnate in such a people all
bring with them a certain homogeneousness, which
brings into being something in the world of thought
forms that you could call the 'spirit' of the people, a
form that is continually fuelled by the individual
citizens. In this way something collective is created
that can exercise a strong influence on the very same
members of a community retroactively.

The factor time in the retroaction of karma

Gradually we are able to imagine a little of how collective and individual karma works. We know that the factor time plays a role too. When questions are asked about the future, the question is nearly always *when* will a certain retroaction occur. Time 'not only heals wounds' but also gives us space to change inwardly, to make new choices and thus influence the retroaction of karma or change the nature of karma. We can nullify or in any case weaken certain karmic incidents, that viewed karmically were waiting for us, by adopting another inner attitude or conviction. Thus we come to be on such 'a different wavelength' that the old karma no longer has a hold on us, is in fact neutralised by our inner change. For the same reason the retroaction concerned might occur in another form. Here again the law of cause and effect meticulously registers the 'energetic change' in us.

Naturally these same laws also apply to world affairs. At this level predictions of future events can fail to come true because large groups of people or humanity as a whole make certain choices.

In the prophecy of the Hopi Indians for example, the chance that the prophecy will not be fulfilled is explicitly left open, if other choices were to be made.[2]

Acceleration and accumulation of events

If we look at the current world situation in the light of the above, we must first of all conclude that a great deal is happening.

Secondly we can ascertain an enormous acceleration in all areas of life.[3] Thus we can ask ourselves why so much is happening and what is causing the general acceleration of the development of this planet.

In the previous section we saw that in addition to individual karma there is also mention of collective karma. This is often stronger than individual karma. Additionally, during the development of mankind on this earth, enormous reservoirs of energy were formed from the power of thought which have been strengthened in the course of thousands of years. There seems to be a self-strengthening process here that is concealing a phenomenal potential. By now it will be clear that an event is not simply an isolated moment but a combination of karmic retroaction, in turn strengthened by similar sorts of energies from the force field, together with choices that people or groups of people make at that moment.

The energies mentioned seek an outlet and find it to a certain extent in the deeds of people on earth. Additionally there are many souls in the beyond, who are temporarily not incarnated at this moment, also searching for an outlet for intense passions or feelings. They also strengthen what is happening on earth. In this way an earth inhabitant who (perhaps unconsciously) is tuned into the 'wavelength love', will flare up with a similar energy. On the other hand someone who harbours a great deal of hate or revenge will make contact with the corresponding force fields. Due to the accumulation of these types of energy in the cosmos over the centuries, in particular the latter type, these now rage as scorching 'fire storms' in many places on earth.

In view of the fact that so much is happening and

so much at the same time, we are also able to perceive an accelerated retroaction. It seems as if the world is under great pressure, or even that time 'is being pushed together' so that retroaction can take place within a very short time. Everything is being brought to light. Things that stayed hidden for years earlier are now ruthlessly submitted for publicity. We only have to think of politics. Corruption and abuse of power is being exposed everywhere and in Italy for instance it appears that even the Mafia, untouchable for decades, is being brought to its knees.

Are we maybe confronted with an event that is bigger than ourselves, that exceeds all historic proportions? Are we perhaps standing on the edge of a sort of apocalyptic phase in human development or are we already in the middle of it?

How did our current situation arise?

Why are we encountering so much alarming unfavourable karma right now? Although looked at spiritually this can be extremely beneficial for our ripening as human beings and in principle should always be considered as an act of love from the Creator.

Man is a 'bipolar' being made up of matter and spirit. We all think that we know what matter is, whereas opinions are immediately divided concerning the spirit. For one person the spirit is connected to the grey substance in our head and thus also to matter. Another refers to the divine source, higher self or self. For me 'spirit' is a non-material 'substance', the innermost core of man, whose origin lies in the 'spiritual sphere'. Essentially man is a descendant from this spiritual realm, a sphere somewhere 'between' the primordial source, God, and the physical world. At that time the spiritual core of man 'descended' from the spiritual sphere, putting on the corresponding coverings (bodies; see chapter 1) during its journey through the various spheres in between, and then finally, many ten thousands of years ago, incarnated on earth for the first time and took on a physical form.

Through his innermost core man could stay in contact with his origin, the higher world, provided he had the right attitude. In addition man also received an instrument on earth in the form of his physical brains and his power of reason, with which he could hold his own in the 'hard' earthly reality.

Both faculties were intended to function together in balance and harmony. Vague memories of his high descent and the awareness of the divine primordial laws should permeate his actions. Actions in which he practically followed his intellect whilst this was guided by his innermost core, his spirit. By doing so he always stayed in harmony with the divine laws and in principle these should only have contributed to his happiness. Karma would have meant: the sweet fruits of his actions.

However, man gradually bound himself more strongly to the material, developed his intellect and the technical knowledge associated with it and neglected his spiritual (intuitive) abilities. Instability entered the world. Man became a predominantly calculating creature always trying to exploit everything to his advantage and was primarily focused on material concerns. Due to his success in the material world he became continually more arrogant and felt himself to be far above the 'poor in spirit', often people it is true who had studied little or were intellectually undeveloped, but who sometimes lived in far greater natural inner harmony with the laws of creation. In the course of this process 'rational man' lost contact with his innermost core and thus with his origin.

Although more strongly accentuated in one culture than in another we actually find this development in all cultures and in all layers of society. The entire human race, with a few exceptions, has chained itself to the material. By doing so it has also severely damaged planet earth. The earth is seriously exploited and polluted at both physical and more subtle levels.

The time will come when the physical earth will react to all the diseases, pollution and mutilation that man has brought to it in just the same way that a body reacts to diseases or poisonous substances.[4] Scientists say that we do not have to worry yet. Climate changes and the like are still falling within the margins of 'the normal'. In view of the many natural disasters and climate swings in the past few years it seems to me that we have landed in the middle of a huge, unavoidable purification process.

If we now consider the ethereal level, we can perhaps imagine that the measure there is full too, that the limits of what is bearable have been reached and that amplified, intensified retroactions occur there too.

What is so special about this time?

Towards the end of a millennium there is often mention of so-called end-of-time thinking. Thus towards the end of the year 1000, people thought that the end of time was approaching. Further we know of ideas such as *kali yuga*, the Iron Age that would end around the year 2000. Without question you will have heard of terms such as New Age, New Time and the Age of Aquarius. The latter will take the place of the Age of Pisces that is now drawing to a close, and spiritually another wind will blow in the world, a spirit of tolerance and cooperation. It is clear that in one way or another many people are living in the expectation that the dawn of a new age is coming closer or has already arrived.

According to many people such transitions are often associated with huge revolutions and natural disasters. The sheer number of events and the speed at which they occur should substantiate the conviction that we are now experiencing such a transition. But what sort of a transition is this then? I believe that at this point in time the human race has to make a very fundamental choice concerning its existence on earth. This is not just another transition from one age to another. In addition to the danger of the (physical) planet becoming totally exhausted and uninhabitable, man is also threatened by a far greater potential disaster on the spiritual level. The gigantic accumulation of 'adverse' karma threatens man in his true self, in his deepest core. I cannot shake the impression that we do not have much more cosmic and possibly earthly time to free ourselves from the 'delusion' of the material.

Isn't it high time that we truly take responsibility for all our thoughts, words, intentions and actions; and that we turn again to the universal laws of creation, and we finally take the place intended for us in the creative scheme?

In the following chapter we will consider the creative scheme in more detail and the role that the universal laws of creation play in it.

—4—

UNIVERSAL LAWS OF CREATION

Who are we? Where do we come from? Where are we going? What is the purpose of our existence? Questions that man has always asked himself and in all probability will continue to ask himself in the future too.

Religions, doctrines, dogmas and science have all formulated answers that have satisfied us to some degree. However we were never completely convinced and continued searching for fresh ideas, for answers that were clearer and better. We had the idea that unity must hide behind the multiplicity, that simple basic patterns might be visible behind the numerous forms that could reduce the multiplicity and diversity of form to simple regularities, and that these could help us to find answers to essential life questions.

In the previous sections several of these 'laws of creation' have been considered. We have seen what an essential role they play in the matter of karma and reincarnation. Before we continue with this discussion let us first take a trip into the past.

Religion or science: who can tell?

Although occasionally serious attempts have been made by both sides to converge, to all intents and purposes science and religion still comprise two separate worlds.

It is well known that science and religion have actually diverged in the western world since the end of the Middle Ages. Before that time science and religion were almost always an extension of each other. The world knew a sort of order that was 'established by God' within which everything fitted neatly. And in those days he who dared to question this order could expect to burn at the stake.

The rationalistic and mechanical view of the world arrived with the Renaissance and continued through the Enlightenment. Reality was no longer interpreted and explained by philosophical and theological (hypo) theses, but could be known through sensory perceptions. On the basis of these perceptions hypotheses were consequently proposed for the course of certain processes in nature. Once these hypotheses were tested and verified man was in a position to propose laws. The nice things about laws, apart from discovering them, was that you could do something with them. You could apply them practically, use them for example to generate or transfer energy (machines). As we know this development eventually led to our current, distinctly technologically oriented society.

Spirit and matter: two separate worlds?

Another phenomenon that can be observed in the same period was a continually deepening specialisation in many fields. As man increasingly immersed himself in the separate parts of reality he lost sight of the larger picture and the underlying cohesion, of the domain of the *uomo universale*, the old ideal of the omnipresent spirit who was able to see the unity behind the multiplicity.

The (external) multiplicity increasingly dominated the experience of modern man, naturally in most situations at the cost of the experience of unity, the mysterious, the religious. At the end of the nineteenth century the sociologist Max Weber spoke of the 'Entzauberung der Welt' (disenchantment of the world). Incidentally it was the same Max Weber who published a study on the relationship between the rise of capitalism and the breakthrough of the Reformation in north-west Europe.

Spirit became an abstraction, a mere collection of mental constructs. For many people spirit and reason have become synonymous, not only in the language but also in their thoughts and actions. Or more truthfully: reason has replaced spirit. The intellect has taken the place of the heart, traditionally the seat of love and feelings.

Spiritual reality was reduced to an abstract reality in our head. It was no longer the invisible dimension behind the visible world, that in fact is just as real as the material world, only the majority of us cannot perceive it because we are now tuned in to a different frequency.

This development also occurred in theology, the science that studies religion. Eventually religion was seen only as an external and social phenomenon and God became a myth or worse still: God was dead.

Towards a new unity

Man has never relinquished his desire for the recovery of the lost unity, for the abolition of the division between the material and spiritual realms and thus of bridging the gap between science and religion. In the Romantic Revival we already find a clear appreciation of the emotional side of human nature, a renewed interest in the stirring of the soul. Around the turn of the century interest in the invisible showed a marked come-back too. Moreover when world events become increasingly turbulent people tend to ask questions to which neither science nor religion can give satisfactory answers.

In the 1920s the businessman Oskar Ernst Bernhardt from Bischofswerda near Dresden gave lectures in many places in Germany. Later under the pseudonym Abd-ru-shin he bundled these together in the book: *Im Lichte der Wahrheit, Gralbotschaft (In the Light of the Truth, The Grail Message)*. He provides answers that appeal to many and that bridge the gap between science and religion, between heart and reason. The laws of creation are an element that constantly reappear in the 168 lectures that constitute the 'Grail Message'. We are already largely familiar with these laws as the laws of nature in the material world. However these laws also operate in the non-material world, the beyond and the higher worlds, albeit in a different form. Abd-ru-shin writes: 'From its very inception the Material Creation was bound to the unalterable Laws of evolution and dissolution; for what we call the Laws of Nature are the Creative Will of God, which in its activity is continually forming and dissolving worlds. This Creative Will is *uniform* in all Creation, to which the Ethereal Worlds and the Gross Material World belong as *one*.'[1] With this the 'Grail Message' revokes the artificial division between what we have called 'spirit' and 'matter' above and thus restores the fundamental unity of creation. We will now look at several examples using the specific laws.

With reference to what was said earlier about the rationalisation and mechanisation of the world, I would like to add here that the 'Grail Message' also suggests that over the course of the centuries man has slowly allowed his reason (-ing brain) to overshadow his inner voice, feeling or intuition. By doing so man has lost his internal rudder and his connection to God and increasingly focuses exclusively on the material. As we have just mentioned, this is a process that is also manifest in science and religion. As a result spiritual and human values have been losing more and more ground to a rational and functional view of life.

Intellect and intuition must once again find a balance – one however in which intuition has authority over intellect, which should be no more than a vehicle. Also (pure intellectual) science should be subordinate to and sustained by our intuition, the connection with the worlds of Light, and thus should be truly subservient to the search for truth and the desire for the noble and good.

Laws of creation

The 'Grail Message' gives a description of the cosmos and within it the place and purpose of human existence. Knowing the creative laws enables us to better understand the workings of the cosmos, why we are here, and how we as human beings can create and improve our own destiny. Time and again it appears that we ourselves are the key to what happens in our lives, that we are included in the universal design and can utilise its effects for our happiness or undoing. We are free in our choices albeit subject to the consequence of those choices. Thus one important creative law has already been stated, that of reciprocal action.

In chapter 2 we saw how important this law is in understanding the logic behind karma and reincarnation. There we were introduced to the law of reciprocal action as the karmic law of cause and effect.

Gravitation

We are all familiar with the law of gravity. Well, something like the law of spiritual gravitation exists too. Human beings become (ethereally) heavier or lighter according to their orientation. On earth we hardly notice the influence of this 'spiritual' gravity because we are all bound by a physical body and thus subject to the same earthly gravitational force. This factor makes earth a unique meeting-place for souls of differing maturity and disposition. This is not possible in the beyond, the ethereal world. There, according to the weight of our ethereal body, we will either 'rise up' to lighter regions or 'sink down' to heavier, darker areas. Our ethereal weight is determined by our orientation, by what we consider to be important in life, by how we feel, think and act. For instance, we automatically become heavier if we have a strong affinity for earthly matters, money or possessions or if we harbour evil desires or feelings of hatred.

We can experience something of this on earth too. In moments of happiness or tranquillity we sometimes experience a sort of 'lightness', conversely we can sometimes feel very 'heavy' when we are really depressed.

Attraction of homogeneous species

We all know that people with a similar disposition seek each other out. 'Like attracts like' as the saying goes. Actually our entire society is under the influence of this law. For instance, we have many forms of association in political, social, religious and occupational areas. Even though our time is characterised by a strong egalitarian tendency, people still join together for certain reasons in our society too. In earlier societies people were guided, largely unconsciously, by this law. They were divided into occupational groups and developmental classes in which everyone had the opportunity to live and develop himself on the basis of similar qualities. Unfortunately later on a class society emerged from this with 'higher' and 'lower' classes that oppressed and fought each other. A truly good application of the law of similar disposition could result in a society in which different classes or groups live *next* to, and with respect for each other, where the diverse dispositions complement each other in lively interaction and together form a whole. This in the realisation that each group is worthy and possesses abilities and talents that the other groups do not have, and thus that each plays an essential role in the larger scheme of things.

Through this law spheres of similarity arise in the beyond, with which we can be connected via our thinking or emotional life. This was considered in the previous chapter.

Under the influence of this law and that of gravity (in the ethereal sense) areas or life spheres are created in the beyond where souls with a similar disposition can 'live together'. In contrast to earth, only souls with the same spiritual disposition and maturity would be found there. There we are also confronted with the imperfections that still cling to us, and thus might have to suffer under the same imperfections of other souls. In the heavier and darker regions it can take a very long time before we become aware of this because we are surrounded only by similarity. As already mentioned this is not the case on earth; there we can 'progress' much faster with our spiritual evolution. This provides a further reason for working on our awareness and spiritual development during our stay on earth. The law of the attraction of homogeneous species also plays an important role in the incarnation of the soul in a physical body.

Here we must make a distinction between the physical inheritance of certain characteristics via the genes and the attraction by the parents of a soul with the same (inner, spiritual) qualities. These two processes actually run parallel but at different levels and complement rather than oppose or exclude one another.

Completion

Plus and minus attract each other. 'Les extrèmes se touchent' as the French saying goes. Doesn't this contradict the law of like-mindedness? In a relationship between two people we always come across the principle of completion and that of like-mindedness. If a lasting and harmonious relationship is to develop the partners should complete each other at the level of qualities and possess a certain degree of agreement, be of a like mind, at the level of convictions. Completion is actually a derivative of the principle of like-mindedness. For example, consider a relationship in which one partner dominates the other. Completion is apparent here because one plays a dominant role in the relationship and the other is satisfied with a subordinate role. Like-mindedness is to be found in the theme 'dominance', both partners representing an aspect of it.

Balance between giving and receiving

This principle should really underpin every human relationship. We should remember that 'it is more agree-able to give than to receive'. We have to give first in order to receive. When we breathe out (give), breathing in (receive) follows naturally. There is no giving with-out receiving, and no receiving without giving.

This law also plays an important role in the exchange between peoples, nations and cultures. One-sidedness can often be observed in this area, together with all the disastrous consequences it produces. In the past too much was taken, now perhaps the wrong things or too much is being given. This law would be a good starting point for the many social institutions and organisations that are so often characterised these days by non-committal anonymity and lack of obliga-tion or overrun by all sorts of contrived bureaucratic commitments.

Movement

'Immobility means degeneration', 'To rest is to rust', expressions that emphasise the importance of keeping moving, both physically and spiritually.

We know too that the universe is not a static entity but consists of constantly expanding and collapsing galaxies in which stars and planets trace their paths, and stars come into existence and fade away again. On earth we also find change and transformation occurring everywhere in nature. Lastly, science has revealed that matter itself is built up of particles that have a wave-like quality, and thus display 'movement'.

Nothing is still, everything is moving. Man must comply with this principle too, otherwise we will stagnate both physically and, at another level, spiritually and eventually get lost in the movement, break up in the vibration.

Movement, for the earth dwellers of this time means enormous acceleration – accelerated incarnations, accelerated karmic retroaction, accelerated change in political and social arenas, accelerated climatic changes. We will be discussing this further in the final chapter of the book.

Movement is the basis for all life, not just in the material world but in all spheres, for without movement creation would not be possible. Movement itself is thus rooted in the creative will of God. In her book *Woorden en Wetten* (Words and Laws), Susanne Schwartzkopff writes: 'Power radiates from God who is Life. This power is transformed into movement. God is the beginning and the end of movement. The entire creation is formed from this; thereby and therein he continues to exist. The power of God flows in this

eternal movement to the tiniest branches of creation
and through every creature, through the leaves on the
trees, through the seemingly lifeless stones. (...) The
foundation of everything is: movement. This keeps
everything fresh and healthy: without movement the
(creative) laws could not exist.'[2]

Laws and inner knowing

We quickly associate the word 'laws' with rigid rules
that limit our freedom to act. I think we are on the
wrong track if a similar thought arises when we discuss
the laws of creation. It would mean being too restricted,
too worldly in our thinking. If we view the creation as
the will and work of God, we can see that the creative
laws, and the associated principles of regularity, flow
directly from this will and work.

Moving on yet one step further, I want to suggest
that we cannot comprehend 'reality' directly (and certainly not intellectually).

What we perceive of reality is an impression, a more
or less subtle or detailed image. Actually our intellect
can only label things, can only produce a very rough,
extremely schematic reproduction of reality.

When we are given an image of a creative law or
when we form one for ourselves, we must fully appre-
ciate that in reality such a law is, on the one hand
infinitely more complicated in its effect, and on the
other hand infinitely more simple in its principle than
we can imagine. The creative laws as presented here
are, as it were, devices with which we can logically
understand reality. The actual underlying principles are
infinitely more lively, subtle and rich. They cannot

really be grasped by reflection but can only be 'sensed' through experience.

Thy will be done ...

In light of the above, the phrase 'Thy will be done', from the Lord's Prayer takes on an entirely new meaning. When we speak these words we are saying that we want to live in accordance with the will of God, that is in accordance with the creative laws. To do this we must first know the laws and make them our own, so that they automatically permeate our thoughts, words and actions like a basic pattern. God speaks to us through His creative laws. That is His language. It is up to us to learn the language.

The 'Grail Message' puts it like this: 'You earthmen are in this Creation to *find* supreme happiness! In the Living Language which God speaks to you! And to understand this Language, to learn it, and to sense inwardly the Will of God in it, *that* is your *goal* during your journey through Creation. In Creation itself, to which you belong, lies the explanation of the *purpose* of your existence, and at the same time also the recognition of your *goal*! In no other way can you find either.

This demands that you *live* Creation. But you are only able to live or *experience* it when you really *know* it.'³

A little earlier in the same chapter: 'The Divine Laws are true friends in everything, they are helpful blessings from the Will of God, Who thus opens the paths to salvation for everyone who strives towards it.'⁴

–5–

CHRISTIANITY, REINCARNATION AND KARMA

Reincarnation and Christianity appeared for many years to be two completely unreconcilable entities. For centuries churches have resolutely rejected reincarnation and persecuted and denounced the followers of the reincarnation doctrine.

It is known that the Church proscribed, among other things, the teachings of church father Origines concerning the pre-birth existence of the soul, and with it thus the possibility of reincarnation. This occurred during the Council of Constantinople (553 B.C.).[1] However, through the centuries belief in reincarnation remained alive in the Christian culture, in spite of the severe persecution of the followers of the reincarnation doctrine.

In the religiously turbulent Middle Ages for example, the renowned Cathars from the South of France professed a faith that came much closer to that of early Christianity and which included a belief in reincarnation.

Later well-known personalities such as Lessing, Goethe, Schiller, Napoleon and many others were convinced followers of the reincarnation doctrine. With the flourishing interest in Eastern religions in the nineteenth century, reincarnation grew quickly in popularity. Spiritual doctrines such as theosophy and anthroposophy, that appeared at the end of the nineteenth, beginning of the twentieth century added to the interest. In ecclesiastical Christian circles there has also been a growing interest in the phenomenon of reincarnation in the last decade. People from a Christian background such as theologian Joanne Klink, author and ex-radio pastor Hans Stolp and the Jesuit Karel Douven speak or have spoken openly about it, based among other things on their experiences with children and terminal patients.[2]

The Bible and reincarnation

There are both supporters and opponents for the opinion that belief in reincarnation was part of the doctrine of Judaism and early Christianity in particular. The supporters say that they have found evidence for the belief in reincarnation during the time of Jesus in several bible texts. According to the Bible Jesus speaks of John the Baptist as the reborn Old Testament prophet Elijah (Matthew 11:14,15) and Jesus's disciples ask why a blind man was born blind: 'Rabbi, who has sinned that he is born blind, this man or his parents?' (John 9:20). It would appear implicitly from these texts that Jesus and his followers were familiar with the doctrine of reincarnation. An assumption that is in agreement with an idea proposed by several sources, including Cayce[3] and Meurois-Givaudan[4], that Jesus belonged to the Essene community which did believe in reincarnation.

Opponents of reincarnation in the Bible state that there is absolutely no evidence of reincarnation in the New Testament, rather that there are texts that oppose the reincarnation idea. For example they point to Hebrews (9:27): 'Everyone must die once, and after that be judged by God. In the same manner Christ also was offered in sacrifice, to take away the sins of many. He will appear a second time, not to deal with sin, but to save those who are waiting for Him'. Of particular interest is the reference to 'dying once'. According to Hans Stolp, from whose book *Karma, reincarnatie en christelijk geloof* (Karma, reincarnation and Christianity) I have borrowed this example, this text relates exclusively to the sole and unique personification of Christ and is not to be seen as an explicit rejection of reincarnation. According to Stolp reincarnation is 'just not a topic of discussion in this text, (...)'[5]. We can however argue on the basis of a similar text that the author, whoever that may be, did *not* proceed from an idea of reincarnation. Evidently we do not get much further by interpreting text from bible passages.

In my view reincarnation, as we now know it, is never really discussed in the Bible, in any case not as a clearly expressed idea, theme or doctrine. However, it might have been removed in the first century of our era. The production of what we now know as the Bible seems to have involved a fairly chaotic process in which much was erased, added and rewritten.[6] Nor is reincarnation for that matter explicitly contradicted. Based purely on what it says in the Bible we cannot say whether

Jesus and his disciples assumed that they had more than one life or not.

Jesus and early Christianity seen in a new light

However, we can find support from another direction for the existence of the reincarnation idea in early Christianity.

Based on the translations of apocryphal texts, such as those found in Nag Hammadi in Egypt, we acquire a view of Jesus and early Christianity that deviates somewhat from the official church view.

To quote Hans Stolp again: 'Through the discovery of the gnostic documents in Nag Hammadi it has become clear that the gnostics formed an important movement in Christianity in the first century (A.D.). Furthermore during the first Christian period the clear cut division between what we would now call orthodox and gnostic Christians did not yet exist. (…) Reincarnation and karma were not unknown to the (Christian) gnostics, they were rather a matter of course. Thus nowadays if one comes to the conclusion that the gnostics formed an inseparable part of early Christianity in the first century, one must also recognise that these insights into karma and reincarnation also had a place in early Christianity. (…) Slavenburg gives several examples of the reincarnation ideas held by the Christian gnostics. He cites church father Irenaeus, quoting from (the school of) Karpokrates: "Before leaving the world the souls must have fulfilled and completed all types of life activity; nothing must remain that still needs performing; otherwise they will be sent back again in another body, because there is still something amiss with their freedom.'"[7]

More of these gnostic text fragments are known. The conclusion that we can draw from the passages above is that the concepts of karma and reincarnation were part of the early Christian body of opinion, perhaps not literally but certainly in spirit, and that with the banishment and the fall into oblivion of gnostic ideas, reincarnation and karma slowly faded into the background in the official Church.

Jesus: love, truth, justice

In our search into the significance of karma and reincarnation for Christianity, let us consider the most pure of Christians, namely Jesus himself. Jesus personifies the core values of Christianity: love, truth and justice. Values that cannot be separated from each other without causing partiality because they keep each other in balance.

Striving for justice without love balancing the action easily leads to harshness. In turn love requires truth (clarity) and justice. If you really care for someone, you must be able to tell him the truth too, even when it is difficult and distressing. What good is love without honesty in a relationship?

The 'Grail Message' puts it like this: 'Genuine love will take no account of what gratifies the other, of what is agreeable to him and gives him joy, but will only direct itself towards what will *benefit* him, regardless of whether it affords him pleasure or not. This is genuine love and service!

If, therefore, it is written: "Love your enemies", it means: "Do that which will benefit them! Punish them if they cannot otherwise be made to understand!" That is serving them! But justice must prevail, for love cannot be separated from justice – they are one!'[8]

To rephrase this concisely, in the first place real love always seeks what is best for the other, meaning that which truly helps him to progress, predominantly inwardly. Real justice is always rooted in and proceeds from this love, and always has the best interest of the other in mind.

It is my impression that Jesus lived by and spoke entirely from these fundamental values, testified by his statements and actions. He was most certainly not the all-accepting, all-pardoning personification of 'divine love', an image that has slowly emerged during the many centuries of church intervention. Acting from his all embracing love he could be extremely strict and uncompromising, simply because this was in the (real) interest of the person in question.

By means of his life Jesus clearly indicated where the balance between love and justice lies, the point at which the balance tips from one side to the other in all sorts of life situations. On the one hand Jesus showed much compassion for the rejected, the poor and the sick. On the other hand he was sharply critical of people's hypocrisy, and not only that of the Pharisees. Jesus was not one to avoid forceful conduct either, bearing in mind the radical manner in which he made short work of the money changers in the temple in Jerusalem.

Nevertheless the image of Jesus handed down by ecclesiastical Christianity is that of a rather meek and mild figure, dispensing love like a shepherd caring for his sheep, the poor sinners. Just take a look at the many portraits that have been painted over the years.

The central dogma of ecclesiastical Christianity, that according to some authors was added later, is one of forgiveness: 'If you believe in Jesus, accept the Lord and show repentance, your sins will be forgiven you and you will enter paradise, whatever you have done wrong.' This doctrine continues to be proclaimed, particularly by the evangelical, missionary groups within Christianity, and in principle the whole of Christendom still accepts it as the foundation of the faith including the redemption that follows from it. We return to the idea of redemption further on in this chapter.

The issue of justice
We have seen above how important it is that love and justice are in balance and both play a role in human actions. Many people quite rightly ask the question, how come there is so much injustice in the world and how is it possible that God, if there is a God, allows it to exist? Indeed for Christianity, in which love and justice have such an important place, this seems to be an extremely legitimate question. How then do divine love and justice operate?

We return again to the concept of karma introduced in chapter 2. My opinion is that karma is *the* answer to the question concerning divine love and justice. The 'law of karma' or 'the law of reciprocal action' is the central law of creation, the way in which God's love and justice finds expression in human existence. I will expand on this below.

As I mentioned earlier karma is simply the repercussion of our thinking, desires and actions. According to the law of reciprocal action we must bear the consequences of our thoughts, endeavours and deeds. These reciprocal actions come our way in the course of time. The law of reciprocal action not only functions at the material level but also in the realm of our thoughts and desires. Retroaction is what we must experience at that moment in order to personally go through what we engendered in the life situation of a fellow man at an earlier moment. Once again: this can be a pleasant or an unpleasant experience, depending on the preceding thought or action.

In Christian circles the law of reciprocal action is sometimes called a 'heartless mechanism of cause and effect'.[9]

Are these critics correct or is the karmic law really a loving application of justice?

At this point the concept of mercy pokes its head around the corner, a term that is often heard in the church too. Mercy is related to forgiveness, exercising kindness towards your enemies or towards those who have done wrong; grace. Once again the right balance between love and justice is involved. Love is however the starting point for mercy.

Is there allusion to mercy (and thus love) in the law of reciprocal action? In my opinion there is: first of all you only have to pay off karma for a particular action once. Thereafter the action is truly forgiven. You will not be blamed for it again years later. Many people have great difficulty forgiving and forgetting and carry around feelings of revenge for many years, even when the culprit has paid for his actions. In fact this creates new karma that will also have to be settled.

Another aspect of mercy in karmic law is the fact

that the retroaction of karma becomes weaker when we change inwardly between the time of the action and the retroaction. The beneficial or painful retroaction will then be experienced less strongly than when the original deed entered the world. An example: in the past a very authoritarian character greatly insulted and humiliated his or her personnel. In the meantime the man or woman has come to see things differently and now has a much more open attitude towards the personnel. When someone truly changes within he can *symbolically* pay off the karma created at that time. The director rolls up his sleeves and helps his personnel where he can so that they can finish an urgent assignment on time. In this way the negative karma from the past can be paid off. The person has changed so much inside, is on such a different 'wavelength' that the energy from the old karma can no longer reach him, cannot take hold of him or in any case has a much weaker effect. We could use the image of the radio receiver tuned into another station.

A third mitigating circumstance by the retroaction of karma is afforded by the 'dosage' in time and quantity. Not all karma comes our way at the same time. In addition, when the 'stars are favourable', weighty karma will have a less undesirable effect on us. We then have time to recover our breath before the next load arrives. Naturally, favourable and unfavourable karma can alternate with each other. It is said that the planet energies form channels for the retroaction of karma. Here we are verging on the terrain of karmic astrology, an area in which I have absolutely no expertise, and which falls outside the scope of this book. I do however find it to be an important aspect of the principle of reciprocal action, because it highlights how it operates with wisdom and love.

Is Jesus really 'the Redeemer'?

In connection with the above we can ask ourselves if we can still view Jesus as our redeemer; this is in fact the crux of ecclesiastical Christianity.

If we personally have to settle what we have brought into the world, how can one man, even if he is very special, how can God himself, deliver us from our 'sins'? This would mean that God acts in variance with his own principles. Besides, should not Judas, as the actual executor of God's 'holy plan' for humanity, actually be revered in all churches?

According to the creative law nothing can be resolved by the 'murder' of Jesus; on the contrary, this is a question of new guilt, new karma, that must also be settled. It is incomprehensible to me that the churches have made this grotesque 'truth', which is in conflict with every fundamental feeling of justice, the centre of their faith.

We ourselves must choose the right path, the way to the light, the truth and life. That is Christ's message. He even gave us an example with his words and deeds and in addition did not even avoid death as a martyr.

The idea that Jesus's death had a redemptive function still holds a great attraction for many people. Even in Christian circles in which people now accept the principles of karma and reincarnation, and within certain spiritual groups (such as anthroposophy), people continue to maintain that the death of Jesus was necessary to enable the individual to settle his karma.[10]

Reincarnation: a fundamental building block

When we further consider our theme from the perspective of the basic complementary Christian principles of love and justice, it is evident that the inclusion of the reincarnation idea in the Christian faith both supports and consummates the essence of Jesus's message rather than undermines it.

If we do not proceed from reincarnation and the closely associated idea of karma, we can presume that there is no such thing as absolute justice. How else can the huge individual differences in wealth, development, talents and circumstances be explained? Considering the world around us, could we continue to talk of a just God or of justice if everything was limited to one life only?

In addition, we established earlier that there is something like the law of reciprocal action, a principle of: man shall reap what man sows. Isn't it strange then that some people only seem to reap bad luck and problems?

We can only comprehend such things when we accept that the seed was sown prior to this life (in a past life) and that the crop (karma) was not harvested at that time. We must also remember that when we sow one grain, we eventually harvest a full ear. This has already been discussed earlier: *every thought, word and deed* that we bring into the world comes back to us multiplied.

Additionally reincarnation presents us with the opportunity of passing through the school of life in several phases, our maturity determining what we have to learn (just like normal school). Certain elements of the study material keep on reappearing until we have mastered them. Many people are continually confronted with the same problem (sometimes in a different guise) in their current life, a problem inevitably connected to their character and qualities. They continue to be confronted with this problem until they have learnt to deal with it in a constructive manner or have attained the maturity to approach it in the right way.

Of what value are these insights to us?

We can conclude that everything that is presented to us in life is intended to assist us with the process of developing our soul, our awareness. Until we have 'learnt our lesson', essentially the same patterns will be placed before us again, albeit in a different form. The realisation that what befalls us in life is a unique and loving helping hand offered by the law of reciprocal action, provides us with courage and confidence based on a logical and clear conviction. With this confidence and conviction we can meet the challenges of life because we *know* that our fate is ultimately in the hands of love, justice and mercy. 'Thus the Laws of Reciprocal Action hold as a great gift of mercy the road to freedom or ascent! Therefore there can be no question of any punishment. Punishment is a wrong expression, for in these laws lies the greatest love – the hand of the Creator stretched out towards forgiveness and liberation!'[11]

About personal forgiveness

The notion of forgiveness has been mentioned several times in this chapter. In the quotation above forgiveness and liberation are mentioned in the same breath. I wish to emphasise here how liberating personal forgiveness can be. We have spoken about the symbolic repayment of karma. I think that one of the most powerful agents influencing this symbolic level is an attitude of real forgiveness towards the people around us. The converse, harbouring feelings of revenge and displeasure, creates karmic links.

First of all we should always be prepared to see our own role in a situation that befalls us, or in something someone does to us. This role must be there, otherwise it would not have happened to us, would it? In what respect were we not mindful enough or did we leave space for this to happen? Secondly we must realise that we resolve nothing with anger and hate, just cause ourselves pain and damage.

An attitude of forgiveness, in the sense of love as described in this chapter, creates space, brings about harmony, heals the soul.

A prospective Christianity

In this chapter I have attempted to show how we can give the Christian faith an entirely new dimension by combining the ideas of karma and reincarnation with the teachings of Jesus, which form the original cornerstone of Christianity.

Continually more people, Christians too, will open up to this 'other perspective' because it provides clear and logical answers to important questions with which we are confronted in life.

In my opinion, if a prospective Christianity is to survive in the future as a viable faith, it must do full justice to the universal principles of love and logic that underpin the concept of karma and reincarnation. Scientific thinking must also base itself on the same principles. Neither Christianity nor science can escape the plea of modern man: formulate an all-embracing and watertight theory about how the world is organised, a model that does justice to both the spirit and the intellect. A Christianity that resorts to all sorts of convoluted theological subtleties in order to explain the world is no more acceptable than a science that denies the existence of anything that is not (yet) weighable and measurable.

Perhaps the religions as we now know them as a sort of power are in fact doomed to die in a future world, in the same way as the crumbling political powers. A future world in which the inner and outer life of people will be guided by the universal cosmic laws.

I am convinced that the same core actually lies locked up in many of the current religions, without doubt coloured by time and the culture within which they exist, but in essence proof of an unchangeable truth that just *is*, unconnected to all human opinions and visions. This is the truth that every Christian, Moslem, Hindu or Buddhist, and perhaps in their heart every atheist too, surely wants to touch if he or she takes life seriously.

–6–

MAN IN CREATION

In the preceding pages we have examined man as an individual, as a (re)-incarnated soul. We have considered the karma that man can accumulate on his journey through materiality and seen how the creative laws can influence his well-being and misfortune. The central question in this chapter is: what place does man have in the creation? Who is he really in relation to God, his co-creatures and nature?

Evolution or creation?

After Darwin published *On the Origin of Species by Means of Natural Selection* in 1859, the scientific world split into two camps: the evolutionists and the creationists.

Based on the ideas of Darwin, the evolutionist concluded that man was the result of gradual development of the 'primordial soup' from molecules via protozoa, invertebrates, vertebrates and mammals to the first primitive man, a sort of glorified ape. This process was steered by a selective mechanism known as the 'survival of the fittest', which implied that only the best adapted individuals could survive. The adaptation originated from spontaneously occurring mutations, changes in the genetic material of the animal or plant concerned. This entire phenomenon was a process that was confined exclusively to the material world. A God, gods or other ethereal, higher beings or a steering mechanism from elsewhere did not enter into it. For many the introduction of this new theory brought the belief about creation into doubt.

In his turn, the creationist maintained that God created the world, according to the 'precisionist' in six days, as laid down in the book of Genesis in the Bible. Others argued that periods of perhaps thousands of years were intended by the days. But it was created. In relation to the text in Genesis we can perhaps ask ourselves if this is indeed a description of material creation. In light of the phrase: 'A thousand years are as one day' (II Peter 3:8), and reflecting on what was said about time and spheres in chapter 1, we could beg the question that the description in Genesis relates to an 'earlier' creation in a 'more rarefied sphere.' Man is created in the image of God, says the Bible; could material creation perhaps also be a reflection of a creation in a higher sphere? Here too: as above, so below?

Adaptation: spontaneous or planned?

First let us examine the idea of evolution more closely. Against the background of the primordial laws of creation, as formulated in chapter 4, we might assume that the 'law of movement' demands that continual development takes place. Immobility means degeneration. Adaptation arises from interaction. By adapting to altered circumstance the species can survive. Thus on the surface the evolutionary principle is not incompatible with the cosmic laws. However, when we ask ourselves how this adaptation comes about, we are immediately faced with another, more essential question, namely: what is nature and how does it function? Are processes in nature entirely independent or are they guided from 'higher', 'finer' levels?

Elemental beings

Let us now take a trip to the barren north of Scotland. A community called Findhorn was started there on an infertile piece of land near to the coast. The thing that makes this community special is that it was set up there at the suggestion of 'elemental beings'. A member of the community, Dorothy Maclean, was able to communicate with *devas*, for normal mortals invisible beings that claim to be responsible for a certain terrain and who supposedly stand at the head of elemental beings of a 'lower' order that care for everything related to nature – from supplying life energy to facilitating germination and growth. Members of Findhorn were not the first to have come into contact with this invisible world of elemental beings and are certainly not the last. The history of mankind is full of stories about men and women who communicated with beings from different spheres. Our early ancestors honoured these beings like gods; unfortunately with the arrival of ecclesiastical Christianity this 'pagan' belief was often opposed with the sword and the flame. Nowadays there are still a surprising number of serious accounts in circulation by people who can sense them or communicate with them.

One such contemporary researcher for example is the Slovenian artist Marko Pogacnik, who describes in his book *Ontmoeting met natuurwezens* (Encounter with nature beings) how he makes contact with this 'invisible' world and increasingly realises how important these beings are for the conservation and restoration of nature and a healthy environment.

My current understanding is, and serious literature in this area is also very explicit, that these beings play an 'essential' role in the development of that particular part of the material world we call nature. At the ethereal level, which 'precedes' the material level, they 'create' or join the forms together which are the blue-prints for this plant or that animal or human body. They guide the entire life cycle from beginning (germination), through growth and flowering, to decomposition of the gross material shell. They also imbue the physical forms with life energy without which the bodies could not come into being, let alone live. In addition they bring about the (energetic) connections between the various essential coverings or 'bodies' of man, as already mentioned in chapter 1.

Steering mechanisms for matter

Returning to our original question: evolution or creation? we can ask ourselves if there could not be a sort of creative plan; a sort of guided development instead of the haphazard chance of genetic mutations? Naturally such an idea would bridge the gap beautifully between those who believe in a creative force and those who argue for purely coincidental, spontaneous processes.

In my opinion the idea of gradual development

(evolution) in itself is far more natural and understand-
able than a 'once only' sort of creative act. Furthermore it is far more in agreement with the findings of
science. However, the principle that lies behind this
gradual development implies far more than that of coin-
cidentally appearing mutations. It implies a process
guided by many 'ethereal beings', both large and small,
all aspiring for perfection.

Glorified animal or a being with divine potential?

What role does man play in all of this? Where does he
stand in this development? Is he, as claimed by scientists, a highly developed, extremely intelligent animal,
or has he divine potential, as many in the New Age
world believe? Or is there perhaps a third alternative
that we have not yet even thought of?

When we look at evolution as it occurred on earth,
in the material, we do indeed see a process from primordial soup to anthropoid ape that lasted millions of
years, although certain links in the chain still appear to
be missing. Viewed from a materialistic-scientific point
of view, man is thus a highly developed animal. Hence
the scientific attempts to develop human skills in
anthropoid apes, to make them, as it were, more intelligent. For science there is not an essential difference
between animal and human, it is rather a matter of
degree. By chance an offshoot of the apes developed
itself further and homo sapiens developed from this
offshoot.

Even though people clearly have 'animal' qualities
(the so-called tribute to nature), I have always had an

aversion to the idea of man as an animal. Not because
I find animals inferior. I actually think that by being
natural, animals fulfil their true nature far better than
humans do. I mean by this that animals are as they are
supposed to be in the creative order. I find that you
cannot always say this for human beings. On the contrary; against his better judgement man often chooses
a way that is at variance with the primordial creative
laws. He has the freedom to do this, which in my view,
the animal does not.

Seen from this perspective humans are definitely
not 'better', but nonetheless rank higher in the creative
order. The expression 'to behave like an animal' is not
intended to discredit the animal but indicates that man
is acting in a way at variance with his original destiny,
with his rightful place in the creative order. But what is
that place?

The divine spark

Let us now examine the two options that I have
proposed. Is man a creature of divine origin, here on
earth in order to so perfect himself that his divine qualities again become visible, with as ultimate goal a sort
of reabsorption into the divine, God? Occasionally the
expression 'divine spark' appears in spiritual literature.
The underlying image here is of an eternal light or fire
that produces sparks. The core of our being is a spark
from that fire, a spark that we can fan into a flame. In
this view we are thus a minuscule particle of God,
derived from Him originally, and split from Him in
order to make a long journey through the universe.
Our assignment would be to bring the divine potential

within us to fruition. It is a tempting thought that appeals to many people nowadays.

The 'Grail Message' takes a forthright stand against the belief that the core of man's being is divine. It says: 'Every man, therefore, who imagines that he bears God within himself or that he is himself Divine, or can become so, lives under a foolish delusion. He bears *spirituality* within him, but *not* Divinity! And therein lies an unbridgeable difference. He is a creature, not part of the Creator, as so many try to make themselves believe. Man is and remains a *work* and can never become a master!'[1]

Just as an artist, the creator of a piece of art, is separate from his work, so is God 'separate' from creation. Man is part of that creation and came into existence somewhere during the course of the creative process. And in the first instance, I am not referring to material man but to spiritual man, to 'spirit-germ' man. In the creative organisation 'a penny can never become a pound', in other words nothing can ever rise above the realm of its origin. If it should rise up, which it cannot, it would 'break up in the vibration', because its constitution or 'maximum frequency' is too coarse for the sphere just above the one from which it came.

We people cannot in fact form an image of God or whatever word we use for that unnameable, rightly undescribable, undefinable 'something'. And that is actually something superbly beautiful. In this way ... gets all his greatness back. We can 'fear' God again (by this I do not mean 'be frightened') and feel holy respect for this greatness. Something that I feel to be special about the human condition is that we can consciously experience this. I do not believe that animals can fear

God consciously. The animal is what it must be and in this sense is in complete harmony with the creative organisation. Man has such a consciousness, that was there in the beginning and that he subsequently developed, that he can consciously place himself outside the organisation, although he is then bound by the consequences of that choice. This makes the human condition unique. This is also why 'freedom' is of such importance to man. In nature you can sometimes experience moments of the greatness of the unnameable at the same time as your own 'humbleness', and also maybe, paradoxically, the enormous freedom of the human condition.

Neither God nor animal

As a human being one can talk of 'higher' and 'lower' in relation to the creative order or organisation in the creation. One might also come to the view that man on earth is, and I emphasise this, *qua origin* closer to the Light than the animals on earth. What then is his relation to the animal? From the physical point of view we have seen that man originates from the animal kingdom. What then constitutes the essential difference between man and animal?

Earlier we already came across several differences that arise from this essential difference. We discussed consciousness and freedom, a conscious human awareness of God. You might say: man stands with one leg in the animal world, in nature and the other in ... where?

Let us turn our thoughts back to a distant past when the earth was still a beautiful paradise and many animals, and ape-like species had developed. It was in this period that a human soul was able to incarnate for the first time. The 'Grail Message' describes it like this: 'Thus the great epoch in the development of Creation had come: On the one side in the Gross Material World stood the most highly developed animal, which was to provide the gross material body as a vessel for the coming man; on the other side in the Ethereal World stood the developed human soul who was waiting to unite with the gross material vessel, and thereby give a further impetus for spiritualisation to everything gross material. Now when an act of procreation took place between the noblest pair of these highly developed animals, there was incarnated at the hour of incarnation not an animal soul, as hitherto, but instead the waiting human soul bearing within it the immortal spirit spark.'[2]

What is described here is in fact the 'evolutionary leap' from animal to human. It was not an animal soul that incarnated but a human soul, 'bearing within it the immortal spirit spark', so concludes the quotation. Notice the choice of words: 'immortal spirit spark'. And earlier in the quotation 'spiritualisation' of everything gross material was mentioned.

Is this not the essential difference with the heretofore incarnated animal souls that are mentioned in this text?

Is this then also the difference between man and animal?

Man: a spiritual being

Man is neither god nor animal but a spiritual being. The concept spirit, as you already know, has nothing to do with intellect or reason, but everything to do with the true nature of man, with the uniqueness of being human.

What is this specific something that makes me human? The beauty I can perceive around me, the deep love I can feel for a person, an animal or the world in which I live. The heartfelt connection that I can enter into with everything outside of me. The gratitude that I can feel for the simple fact that I exist. But also the deep sadness at the loss of a loved one. The existential loneliness of man. All this and much more makes me human. An exceptional characteristic of being human, perhaps the most distinctive, is an awareness of higher things, a notion of God. This notion of God must have something to do with his inner being, with the spiritual core of which we spoke earlier. A passage from the 'Grail Message' might offer clarification. 'There is within you an altar which should serve for the worship of your God. This altar is your intuitive faculty. If this is pure it is directly connected with the Spiritual Realm and thus with Paradise! Then there are moments when you too can fully perceive the nearness of your God, as often happens in times of deepest sorrow and greatest joy!'[3]

We can read something very important here. Our intuition is apparently our bridge to higher things and at the same time also something of a connection with our origin, the spiritual realm. However, we must keep it pure, free of 'dirt' in order to 'receive' effectively.

Is it not this kind of experience, the sensing of the source of all existence, that the mystics Jacob Boehme, Hildegard van Bingen and Erik van Ruysbeek have written about? It will be clear from the words just quoted and from the tone of this book that the only emotion this brings about in man is an overwhelming 'feeling of love'. Suddenly the world falls into place and the natural order becomes clear. This capacity for insight, an insight that goes beyond the physical limitations of being human and that reminds man of his origin, this is his spiritual inheritance. Only then is he human.

A distant call
A symphony of light
from a source far away

Longing for destiny
for a purpose
for a reason

A sound
crosses
the void

A bird
flies
into the distance

Searing blaze
simmers in the soul
Consuming fire
rages in the heart
Red

Sunlight shines still
through the droplets
The laugh of the rainbow
warms the heavens

Fragile stillness
is ethereally
perceptible
Morning has broken![1]

EPILOGUE:

THE INSATIABLE LONGING

'An inconceivably long time ago, a great train of bright little flames went forth from their Eternal Home, where a delicate breath of spring had only just awakened them out of a deep sleep. Many a luminous hand was raised in blessing, as though in a last greeting, and loving, kindly glances followed after them.

The bells of Paradise were ringing as they departed, and even at the last moment they caught this silver-clear tone, and cherished it deep in their young hearts. Then the little points, whirling merrily, sank into the world-embracing depths.'[1]

The journey as metaphor

We travel because it is a pleasure to do so. We flock in our thousands to distant holiday destinations, ski down snowy mountains in the winter in our hundreds or book 'ecological' excursions by plane to Tierra del Fuego or the Brazilian rain forests.

Back home again, after spending a considerable part of the working day sitting behind a desk or in the car, we jog or follow fitness classes in specially designed sport schools. It appears that we have an enormous desire to move, a longing that needs satisfying, but that often can no longer be fulfilled in our over-civilised existence.

Where does this desire to move come from? Upon which personal motives and processes does it depend? Is there perhaps more behind our great need to move, to make long journeys to the most exotic destinations?

What are the internal patterns behind all this journeying, the psychic blueprint of this enormous desire for movement, for activity?

The journey of the artist

In the seventeenth, eighteenth and nineteenth centuries many artists and writers took a trip to Italy: P.C. Hooft from The Netherlands, Goethe from Germany and Turner from England to name but a few. In those days Italy was perceived as the Mecca of culture and refinement, the land in which the Renaissance was rooted and the classics had left their mark. Cities such as Florence, Venice, Siena, and of course Rome were important destinations.

Travelling in those days was far more perilous and demanding than now. One travelled by ship, stagecoach, horse or foot and was exposed to many dangers on the way. The world then was less densely populated, there were fewer roads, highwaymen lay in wait everywhere and the chance of being attacked and robbed was not unreal, particularly in inhospitable and uninhabited areas; one was also far more dependent on the weather than nowadays. Thus a journey to Italy was a real undertaking. But also a marvellous experience. Aside from the eagerly desired destination, the trip itself was a source of inspiration for the artist. Now he passed by and through walled cities, through the lovely gardens of the European landscape strewn with vineyards, fields, meadows, with the occasional lonely castle or remote cloister, safe resting places on a sometimes barren journey. Then his journey continued for days through lofty trees, pine forests or remote mountain landscapes. And finally he came to behold the southern light, and to savour the sweet warmth of Tuscany. Was Johann Wolfgang Goethe referring to this land when he lets Mignon lament in *Wilhelm Meister*:

> 'Kennst du das Land, wo die Zitronen blühn,
> Im dunkeln Laub die Gold-Orangen glühn,
> Ein sanfter Wind vom blauen Himmel weht,
> Die Myrte still und hoch der Lorbeer steht
> Kennst du es wohl?
> Dahin! Dahin
> Möcht'ich mit dir, o mein Geliebter, ziehn.'[2]

It was, perhaps, a journey in more than one sense of the word, a search for the light, not only for the light of the 'south', but also for an inner light, perhaps for enlightenment, for an inward perfusion of the light of art and culture.

'Make way, make way, make way... we have no time to stay!'[3]

When we look at the world today we see a totally different world to that of Goethe. For many people modern society is like a sort of prison, a corset of responsibilities. Thus many yearn for freedom, to be unshackled, to be liberated from the endless daily routine of clock and calendar. We do not feel that we have 'oceans of time' for ourselves, in spite of the increased leisure time in Western society.

The factor time is playing an increasingly more important role in our experience. People want to do as much as possible in as little time as possible – an interesting phenomenon. We also find it difficult to make choices between things and would like nothing better than to be everywhere, and to do everything, simultaneously. For example we want children and to keep working full-time, we want to build a house and take a three-week holiday. We can elaborate further: at intellectual and spiritual levels people also want to profit from, participate in, trends and developments in the society.

Everything must be faster, more efficient and better. But the question remains: why? The answer is: otherwise 'the competitor' outstrips us! Thus 'market thinking' has infiltrated, not only our economy where it belongs, but our whole existence. The 'market virus' has settled into our consciousness.

As I see it, many people live in terms of productivity, money and time, in their private lives too.

Externalisation

Sometimes the thought occurs to me that we do many things at a level other than the level for which they were intended. For example, consider the computer and communication devices now available. Why haven't we developed the functions that these devices offer at a different level? Why aren't we precognitive and why don't we communicate telepathically instead of needing equipment to do this? If there is some kind of development plan underlying the existence of man on this earth, isn't the intended development taking place at too 'low' a level? The form exists but the content appears to be a surrogate of lesser quality. The production of chips requires a perfectly clean environment and silicon of very pure quality. This ensures that absolutely no impurities can enter the finished product during its production as this could lead to possible disruption in data storage or processing in the computer memory later on. This is particularly important in view of the degree of miniaturisation.

Someone once suggested the idea that we too pursue a lower level of pureness than we perhaps ought too. If we tried to achieve inner purity with the same dedication, wouldn't the world be more trouble-free at that level than it is today?

If you place these thoughts in historical and social perspective, and consider how many impulses man has had, and then look at the final outcome of these impulses, you can see that the, in themselves, noble motives and high ideals often got turned in the wrong direction and found a purely materialistic form of expression in historical and social reality. Symbolically you could compare this to the biblical story of the Golden Calf. The offering of the unnameable was displaced, translated into a concrete effigy in the wilderness, moulded from gold jewellery, symbol for the best that man could give of himself.

Closer to home and our own era, we can recall the way in which the Nazis turned human ideals and qualities into insane ideas and dreadful actions. At that time, perhaps even more so in that time, a longing to mean something to the world, the yearning for a new time of peace and prosperity for all, must have existed in the people. An optimism that was partly supported by the great achievements in science and technology during the first decades of the twentieth century. This might explain why the ideas were unconditionally accepted by large groups both within and outside German society.

In twentieth century society we see a general tendency towards a more hurried and superficial way of living, particularly visible in external forms that continue to take on a more material and lifeless character. In numerous cultural expressions: art, photography, advertisement; a good measure of certain, often unconscious, trends in society; the taut, hard, stylised, perfect but cold and lifeless prevails over the loose, soft, irregular, imperfect but warm-blooded life. These days the imperfect picture can be made perfect by using digital manipulation. Are we aiming for purity here at the wrong level too?

The need to be in motion

We all know that we become stiff if we sit for too long in a chair. Eventually muscles atrophy if we do not use them; joints stiffen if they are rested for too long. Movement is absolutely essential for maintaining certain functions in the body. In nature we can observe how systems generally tend towards equilibrium, that is *move* towards a stable state. However, because external factors are always influencing such systems the stable status quo is never achieved. Thus a system must constantly be in motion if it is to survive.

Movement, flexibility and adaptability are vital conditions for every living organism. As we have seen, the evolutionary concept is in fact based on this principle; organisms that are unable to adapt, do not survive.

Movement is absolutely essential at the inner level too. *Having* to move, having to choose, is inherently human. Life is indeed a sort of journey with choice moments emerging at every turn, crossroads at which we must choose a direction if we are to move on. Although this metaphor might seem exaggerated, we realise on closer examination that we make such choices nearly every minute of the day. Even the decision not to make a choice is still a choice!

In my opinion, the aspect of 'having to' is closely related to the law of movement that we observe not only in external phenomena, as mentioned above, but that we also encounter at the spiritual and psychological level in ourselves. How often do we evaluate things, more or less consciously or unconsciously, by asking ourselves: was that useful to me? Have I made headway or developed in any way? Or more philosophically: how was that meaningful to me?

Seemingly we perceive 'getting somewhere' as a must, an autonomous principle, in the same way that grass or trees always grow towards the light. Clearly we always *want to go somewhere*.

The artist hankering for the horizon, the jogger working on his condition, and the tourist making long journeys all have something in common. They all long for a condition that seems to be more desirable to them than their current state.

Thus inwardly we are literally continuously moving

from A to B, you could say travelling, during everything that we do.

A good example of how this hypothesis unconsciously preoccupies us is the so-called 'belief in progress'. Many are of the opinion that the enormous progress made within science and technology in the last hundred years is based on this belief. Objectively seen (in so far as this is possible) this view can be challenged on several points.

Traveller between yesterday and tomorrow

We people are travellers between yesterday and tomorrow, with a consciousness that has difficulty living in the present, that is inclined to linger in the past, or long for a future that maybe never appears. And yet our existence, as we have established, is an endless succession of todays, of nows, of moments in which we must constantly choose our direction. Regardless of how we do it, we are on the move, on our way to somewhere. Often we do not know whereto.

Seen like this the journey is also a metaphor for inner processes: it seems that we sometimes attach more value to capturing the perceived reality on film or video (the past) than to the innermost experience of the moment itself. We prepare ourselves by studying the area which we will be visiting (the future) in order to look around in the most efficient way possible. Back home again we can re-experience (the past) the event with photographs and video films. The question remains, where was our consciousness during the moment itself (the present)? Because this is what it is about, is it not? It is not the photographs, not the well-laid plans that matter, it is our soul that matters, the journey that we make with our soul. At least it would be if we accept that the things that we truly intimately experience are the only things that we can actually take with us, the only things that really matter to our being, to our core. Even here it often seems that we are only concerned with the surface of things.

Is it any surprise that external movement has replaced internal movement in a strongly externalised society in which speed and usefulness take priority? Is the gigantic need to move at the material level not a compensation for a lack of internal movement? Is the plane journey to that far-off land a replacement for the inner journey we forgot to make? Is the fullness of our agenda perhaps equal to the inner emptiness that we try so hard to escape?

And does the restlessness and the continual searching, which expresses itself so strongly in our need for constant distraction and variety, for a change of scenery, for 'a few days away', suggest that we are looking for something that we have lost, something quiescent, deep in our conscience, a vague memory, a remote call?

The unappeasable, redeeming desire

The image that slowly emerges is that of a driven man, essentially searching for his core, his origin, or whatever you wish to call the aim of the inner longing.

Many feverishly attempt to quieten this longing in the outside world because they are unfamiliar with the notion of a real inner world, a true spiritual, intangible reality. Consciousness is for them no more than a physical mass of brain cells, the evolutionary product of a coincidental convergence of circumstances.

Steadily, more and more people are becoming aware that they have a need for a new dimension, a 'broader' picture of reality than the purely scientific, materialistic viewpoint. They refuse, for example, to accept that certain human qualities can be expressed in purely biological terms. Man is more!

Are we not in all our restlessness and desires really searching for that 'something more', for that 'something more' that we as human beings can be? With the emphasis on 'can'. You only need to look around you to see that it is not always apparent that we are this. Isn't this distant call, this vague memory, both evidence and a reminder of our origin, that simultaneously incorporates our vocation, our mission?

The circle closes. If we reread the quotation at the beginning of the chapter we learn that the beginning of every movement, every journey is actually anchored in that unappeasable yearning for a land which we once left, for the 'mother' from whose lap we came.

Perhaps all the unrest, the need to move, the desire to experience a myriad of things, the wish to do everything simultaneously and the lack of time associated with this, is also an (unconscious) signal that we should hurry up, that time is of the essence, that it is high time we gave attention to the journey, the journey of our soul, and perhaps more important still, to the final destination ...

Let us not stifle this unappeasable yearning, let us cherish it as a priceless treasure, as our link with the beyond. If it reveals itself, let us listen to it, however soft its voice. It is, after all, our lifeline, our anchor in eternity.

CODA

Our 'journey' together, dear reader, is almost over. We experienced a great deal on the way. I hope that you too enjoyed the beautiful scenes that we saw, the wonderful music that we heard, the poetry that softened our hearts, and that finally satisfied, you were able to let go of the difficult moments that we had together.

There were difficult moments for me too, troublesome questions that I perhaps could not answer to my own or your satisfaction, in which I was not sufficiently exhaustive. For the writer of a book his product is no more than a snapshot of his insights and his ability to communicate them.

I hope that I have succeeded in conveying something of the best and most valuable, from which, up until now, I have benefitted so much myself. This was my only wish.

NOTES

CHAPTER 1

1. Taken from H. van Praag, *Reïncarnatie*, p. 18 ff.
2. See Van Lommel, *Bijna-doodervaringen*.
3. See Abd-ru-shin, *In the Light of Truth, The Grail Message*, Vol. 2, p. 19
4. H. Motoyama, *Karma and Reincarnation*, p. 16
5. See Abd-ru-shin, *In the Light of Truth, The Grail Message*, Vol. 2, p. 356 'as is the case today with our part of the world where only souls can live which have already been incarnated several times'.
6. Taken from J. van Auken, *The End Times*.
7. Taken from H. van Praag, *Reïncarnatie*, p. 34 ff.

CHAPTER 2

1. See also Corrie ten Boom, *The Hiding Place*.
2. See Abd-ru-shin, *In the Light of Truth, The Grail Message*, Vol. 2, p. 47–48. For a broader introduction to this book see chapter 4.

CHAPTER 3

1. H. Motoyama, *Karma and Reincarnation*, p. 61–62
2. See R. Kaiser, *Die Stimme des grossen Geistes*.
3. By these means souls also incarnate faster, which, seen from the reincarnation perspective, could explain the rapid growth in the world population.

4. Those who want to know more about the parallels between the earth and the human body can read R. Dahlke, *Der Mensch und die Welt sind eins*.

CHAPTER 4

1. Abd-ru-shin, *In the Light of Truth, The Grail Message*, Vol. 1, p. 71
2. S. Schwartzkopff, *Woorden en wetten*, p. 25
3. Abd-ru-shin, *In the Light of Truth, The Grail Message*, Vol. 1, p. 201–202
4. Abd-ru-shin, *In the Light of Truth, The Grail Message*, Vol. 1, p. 201

CHAPTER 5

1. See N. Langley, *Edgar Cayce on Reincarnation*, p. 179 ff.
2. See books by Klink and Stolp in the bibliography.
3. See N. Langley, *Edgar Cayce on Reincarnation*, p. 153 ff.
4. A. & D. Meurois-Givaudan, *De mémoire D'Essénien*.
5. H. Stolp, *Karma, reïncarnatie en christelijk geloof*, p. 44
6. A revealing account of the historical origin of the New Testament can be found in B. Mack, *Who wrote the New Testament?*
7. H. Stolp, *Karma, reïncarnatie en christelijk geloof*, p. 47 ff. The quote by Slavenburg is taken from Margreet van den Brink et al, *Karma en reïncarnatie, vroeger, nu en in de toekomst*, p. 12
8. Abd-ru-shin, *In the Light of Truth, The Grail Message*, Vol. 2, p. 37
9. J. Verkuyl, *Antroposofie en het evangelie van Jezus Christus*.

10. For this view see: M. van den Brink et al, *Karma en reïncarnatie, vroeger, nu en in de toekomst*.
11. Abd-ru-shin, *In the Light of Truth, The Grail Message*, Vol. 2, p.48

CHAPTER 6
1. Abd-ru-shin, *In the Light of Truth, The Grail Message*, Vol. 2, p. 176
2. Abd-ru-shin, *In the Light of Truth, The Grail Message*, Vol. 2, p. 19
3. Abd-ru-shin, *In the Light of Truth, The Grail Message*, Vol. 1, p. 104

POEM (page 92)
1. Ralph Vaughan Williams, 5th Symphony; verbal impression of the author.

EPILOGUE
1. From H. Vollmann, *What lies behind it*, p. 40
2. Translation (by the author)
   Do you know the land of flowering lemon trees,
   Where golden apples glow between the darker leaves,
   A soft breeze blowing across the blue sky,
   The myrtle silent and the laurel reaches high
   You know that land?
   Thither! Thither
   I wish to go, my love, with you!
3. From a song by Herman van Veen, *Opzij*.

BIBLIOGRAPHY

Abd-ru-shin, *In the Light of Truth, The Grail Message*, Stuttgart 1990.

Abd-ru-shin, *The Ten Commandments and the Lord's Prayer*, Stuttgart 1982.

J. van Auken, *The End Times*, Virginia Beach 1994.

Corrie ten Boom, *The Hiding Place*, Hoornaar

M. v.d. Brink, *Karma en reïncarnatie, vroeger, nu en in de toekomst*, Zeist 1995.

G. Cerminara, *Many Mansions*, London 1971.

R. Dahkle, *Der Mensch und die Welt sind eins*, Munich 1987.

C.P. Flynn, *After the Beyond; Human Transformation and the Near-Death Experience*, Englewood Cliffs 1986.

H.P.M. Goddijn et al, *Geschiedenis van de sociologie*, Meppel 1974.

S. Hagl, *Die Apokalypse als Hoffnung*, Munich 1988.

R. Kaiser, *Die Stimme des grossen Geistes; Prophezeiungen und Endzeiterwartungen der Hopi-Indianer*, Munich 1989.

J. Klink, *Vroeger toen ik groot was*, Baarn 1990.

R. Kranenborg, *Reïncarnatie en christelijk geloof*, Kampen 1989.

R. Kranenborg, H.S. Verbrugh et al, *Reïncarnatie, een veelzijdig perspectief?*, Kampen 1988.

S. Lampe, *The Christian and Reincarnation*, Wolverhampton 1990.

N. Langley, *Edgar Cayce on reincarnation*, New York 1967.

P. van Lommel et al, *Bijna-doodervaringen*, Deventer 1996.

B.L. Mack, *Who wrote the New Testament? The Making of the Christian Myth*, San Francisco 1995.

A. & D. Meurois-Givaudan, *De mémoire D'Essénien; l'autre visage de Jésus*, Plazac/Rouffignac.

A. & D. Meurois-Givaudan, *Les neuf marches; histoire de naître et de renaître*, Plazac/Rouffignac.

R.A. Monroe, *Journeys out of the Body*, Garden City (NY) 1973.

R. Moody, *Life after Life*, Covington (GA) 1975.

H. Motoyama, *Karma and Reincarnation*, London 1992.

M. Pogacnik, *Elementarwesen; die Gefühlsebene der Erde*, Munich 1995.

H. van Praag, *Reïncarnatie in het licht van wetenschap en geloof*, Bussum 1972.

S. Schwartzkopff, *Woorden en wetten*, Breda 1995.

J. Slavenburg, *De verborgen leringen van Jezus*, Deventer 1992.

J. Slavenburg, *Een ander testament*, Deventer 1991.

C. Snow, *Mass-dreams of the Future*, New York 1989.

R. Steinpach, *How is it that we Live after Death and What is the Meaning of Life?*, Stuttgart 1989.

I. Stevenson, *Twenty Cases Suggestive of Reincarnation*, New York 1966.

H. Stolp, *Kijk, maar kijk in verwondering*, Baarn 1990.

H. Stolp, *Karma, reïncarnatie en christelijk geloof*, Baarn 1996.

J. Verkuyl, *Antroposofie en het evangelie van Jezus Christus*, Kampen 1986.

Bibliography

H. Vollmann, *What lies behind it*, Stuttgart 1977.

M. Weber, *Die protestantische Ethik und der Geist des Kapitalismus*, 1905.

K. Zoeteman, *Gaia-Sophia; a Framework for Ecology*, Edinburgh 1991.

If the reader would like to contact the author, he or she can do so by writing to him at the following address;

Albert Bodde
c/o Uitgeverij Ankh-Hermes,
Postbus 125,
7400 AC Deventer,
The Netherlands

fax: 00 31 570 624632

e-mail: ankh-hermes.nl@wxs.nl

Further information on the 'Grail Message' can be obtained from:

Grail Acres Publishing Company,
23B Hamilton Road,
Sidcup,
Kent, DA15 7HB
United Kingdom

telephone: (020) 8309 0379

fax: (020) 8309 7105

e-mail: gapc@compuserve.com

Website: www.gral.de

INDEX

116

Index